"I devoured her book and ↑
writing class, I knew I had
craft and creates such a war... ... welcoming atmosphere, that you
feel empowered, encouraged, and enlightened! Linda is a master at
demystifying the process. You will leave her class feeling unstop-
pable!"
— Tom Sheeter, Writer

"Linda Bergman's book gave me the inspiration to start writing. In
four years, I have completed 2 features, (one a Nichols Fellowship
Quarter-Finalist), and a pilot. I took her workshop and I found it
invaluable. Witnessing her knowledge and wisdom is an experience
no writer should miss."
— Stefanie Kahn, Screenwriter

"As a veteran of various Bergman screenplay sessions, and several
of her memoir series, I've seen motivated people leave a ten-week
session with the better part of a script in hand. And in these finely
tuned classes, the synergy of working with other students and their
scripts will enhance your own."
— Marilyn Fuss, Educator

"Linda Bergman is a spectacular workshop leader. She presents with
a lightning thrust of creativity, insight and humor. I've read her wonderful book, attended her class, and have emerged with a new way
of looking at film and script writing. Bravo, Linda!"
— Geri Lennon, Author, Biomedical researcher

"Being in Linda's company is inviting and inspiring. It is a warm and
supportive atmosphere. You walk away saying, "I can do this!"
— Paul Chepikian, Writer/Editor/Filmmaker

"Linda Bergman's book and workshop taught me about plot, structure, and character in a way that has benefited my writing in
every area—fiction, screenwriting, and nonfiction. I would highly

recommend both to anyone interested in learning how to construct a great story."

—Dixie L. King Ph.D.

"Linda is smart, funny, and insightful, and her class was a joy to take. She gave me a lot of 'aha" moments and now I'm beating out the rewrite of my screenplay. I highly recommend both her class and her book."

—Anne Hikido, Writer/Health Professional

SO YOU THINK YOUR LIFE'S A MOVIE?

The Sequel

LINDA BERGMAN

Bergman Entertainment. Inc.
13333 Ventura Blvd. Ste 201
Sherman Oaks, CA. 91423
818-788-8192

101 Greatest Film Screenplays of All Time ©WGA
Sarah Forever Screenplay Copyright © 2011 Linda Bergman.
Toot Toot Tootsie Goodbye Screenplay Copyright © 2011 Linda Bergman & Martin Tahse based on the novel by Ron Powers.
How Do I Get An Agent? Copyright © 2011 Nuvotech Limited

Library of Congress Cataloging-in-publication Data is available
ISBN 978-0-9834650-2-7(pb)   ISBN 978-0-9834650-3-4 (e)

1. Screenplay 2. Entertainment   1. Title

2011904871

Printed in the United States of America First printing, April 2016

Book Design by Karrie Ross www.KarrieRoss.com
Linda Bergman's Write of Passage logo designed by Kristina Phillippe
www.Phillippedesigngroup.com
Back cover photo by Paul Chepikian

www.Bergmanentertainment.com
www.soyouthinkyourlifesamovie.com

ACKNOWLEDGEMENTS

A huge gift in each of our lives is the awareness that we learn and transform through our experiences. In honoring my passion for the art of making movies, I am pleased to bring my newest experiences to the table in *SO YOU THINK YOUR LIFE'S A MOVIE – THE SEQUEL.*

John Sacret Young, producer, director, writer (*China Beach*) once said to me on the Warner Brothers lot, "Facing the blank page is like jumping into an abyss. And if you ever do hit bottom, you have to dig deeper." This advice made a huge impact on me. He taught me, as did my other teachers, that good writing is rewriting and rewriting and rewriting. Did I mention rewriting?

In the last five years, I have learned even more about digging deeper from my own writing experience, from a special Pulitzer Prize winning writer, Ron Powers, (*Flags Of Our Fathers*) and from student feedback in my classes. To up my game, I've read and seen five more years of Academy Award winning screenplays and broken them down to see how their structure fits into the three act paradigm. I'm happy to share all that's new for me – with you.

But, wait. Not all is new. I have corrected typos and punctuations and repaired an embarrassing case of misinformation, but kept many of the pearls from the first edition. You'll find I've substantially added new gems to the string of examples, insights and technique. And I've left the chapter movie quotes the same because they all still make me laugh!

Thank you to all the men and women who have inspired me and/or hired me over the years: Jim Green, Allen Epstein, Marc Bacino, Faye Kanin, Peter Guber, Valerie Harper, Sid Ganis, Bruce Vinokour, Tony Cacciotti, Sid Ganis, Elizabeth Yost, Barbara Mandrell, Ken Dudney, Maureen McCormick, Ron Powers, Eve Wasserman, Jerry London, Betty Egan, Jon Ringquist, Blair Brown, Marion Anderson, Pearl S. Buck, Sela Ward, Jill Clayburgh, Lillian Gallo, John Sacret Young, Jessica Savitch, Dolly Parton, Jane Seymour, Martin Tahse, John Egan, Jim Dennett and Penny Fuller.

Some of these names may be familiar to you and many who work behind the scenes are not. In gratitude, I profess, "It takes a village" to make a movie and I have been lucky to have resided in many. I'd like to say thank you to all the villagers, past, present and future for sharing your gifts and brightening my life with your light.

To all my readers and students, thank you for jumping into the abyss with me. Oh, and by the way,

"You had me at Hello." *Jerry McGuire 2006*

With Love and Deep Gratitude to

My husband, Chuck Bergman,
my daughter, Sarah Bergman Zenoff,
and my son, Adam Bergman
for their fine minds and open hearts and
for supporting me at every
curve on the path.

TABLE OF CONTENTS

INTRODUCTION

I was born in a factory town. In Los Angeles we weren't making cars like they did in Detroit or steel like they made in Pittsburgh. We assembly-lined television shows and movies. Many of the kids in school were born to famous parents or were famous themselves – Sally Field and Cindy Williams come to mind. I mean, really. With "Gidget" and "Shirley Feeney" in my lunch lines, and Clint Eastwood swimming in my pool, I thought anything was possible.

I did start to take drama classes but more importantly for the journey I was about to take, I began to write. My first play, "The Boy Prince" was put on its feet the summer I was eleven and lasted all of six minutes. My brother, Richard, was to play the Prince but my best girl friend down the street was taller. Her mother donated home-made lemonade and chocolate chip cookies so I bent gender without a blink. And the daughter of the handsome actor Bill Hopper (*Perry Mason*) did our make-up, so his presence insured us a celebrity audience of one.

Buoyed by Sue Bauer, my English teacher at Birmingham High School in Van Nuys, I worked at becoming a more serious scribe. Because of the volatile nature of our home, my brother and I had a no-talk rule and so I would write my unexpressed feelings in a notebook for Miss Bauer to read. Her margin notes became my path out of the dark and her fiction assignments helped my imagination take wing.

In my first television project, an ABC After School Special titled *Just Tipsy, Honey* produced by Martin Tahse, I offered an homage to her. I created a character named "Miss Bauer" who was a supportive teacher to a teen with an alcoholic mother. Martin and I cast my best friend, actress Kathryn Skatula, and I was giddy with joy on the first day of shooting. Though it was a reminder of a very tough time growing up, my family strife actually supplied the material for my first job and thus the credentials to keep getting hired.

After high school, I was at UCLA studying communications to prepare me for film school when a neighbor hired me to work for Fouad Said who was revolutionizing the entertainment industry. He had created the Cinemobile, a bus-like vehicle that facilitated the transport of film equipment to location shoots.

I Spy was the first TV series shot in various locations around the world because of the ease in which the Cinemobile could be shipped. We sent it via the Guppy, a wide-bodied cargo aircraft built for ferrying NASA's components of the Apollo program. It didn't just revolutionize an industry, it turned me upside down. At Cinemobile, I didn't write but learned a myriad of other skills — negotiating the rental of equipment, writing production reports and preparing production payroll – skills that would soon come into play in the profession that was choosing me.

I met a number of producers and directors who would influence the way I began to look at films. I began to see them from behind the scenes rather than in front of them. Sean Penn's father, director Arthur Penn (*Little Big Man, Bonnie and Clyde, The Miracle Worker*) stands out as does Sheldon Leonard (*I Spy, Make Room for Daddy, The Dick Van Dyke Show*), Sam Peckinpah (*The Wild Bunch, The Ballad of Cable Hogue*) and his co-producer, Bill Farella. Bill swiped me right out of my chair, doubled my salary, and took me with him to Twentieth Century-Fox. At 21, I was almost "in the movies!"

On my first day, the studio looked like a ghost town. I drove down the *Hello Dolly* New York Street (a last testament to what was arguably the end of Hollywood's musical golden age) and parked where Dolly marched side by side with Horace and where she taught Cornelius and Barnaby how to dance.

I naively asked the guard at the gate why it was so quiet. Of all the notorious celebrity deaths, suicides, and murders that have happened throughout Hollywood history, none was as bizarre and gruesome as the murders that occurred the night before in Benedict Canyon, a hilly suburb of Los Angeles. A young, pregnant Sharon Tate and four of her houseguests had been brutally murdered.

Sharon Tate was under contract to Fox at the time and the guard was quick to gossip. The word on the street was that it was a conspiracy against the studio and that, one by one, all Fox employees would die. No wonder everyone stayed home! It would take months before Charles Manson took credit for the murders. Since my new boss, Bill Farella, wasn't afraid of anything, I showed up to work as ordered to help him make a movie for television called *Along Came A Spider* starring Suzanne Pleschette.

I was bright and hungry to learn, so Farella, deep into his sixties, took me under his wing. He was a big, tough, Irish-Italian with a white handle-bar moustache who expected as much from the people who worked for him as he expected of himself. He had already fired twenty-nine people for Sam Peckinpah. Everyone down to the electricians came to work knowing they were expected to read the script and dedicate themselves to the picture. If they didn't, they were gone. Farella could be as mean as a junk-yard dog but he liked me and after a fast game of gin each morning he'd teach me something invaluable.

Besides learning to "take my lumps" when I screwed up, he showed me how to break down a script into a production strip board — a wooden chart holding color-coded strips of paper, each containing information about a scene in the script. The strips could then be rearranged and laid out sequentially to represent the order in which scenes could be filmed. This produces a schedule that the producers can use to plan the production. You knew what actors were in each scene, where it was filmed, whether it was day or night, what special effects and props were needed and how long it was by the page count. In doing this, I learned quickly which scenes in a movie were irrelevant even before filming began. Even though it was a production skill for me, it was script writing 101.

After the movie wrapped, I was tossed into the steno pool at Fox where I typed scripts until someone else needed an assistant. I remember typing page after page thinking, "I can do better than this." I was a sponge. I learned about pace and rhythm and that the main purpose of dialogue is to move the story along. I saw what was cut from the original versions of the script to make scenes tighter and more comprehensive. Those days were exciting. When I went to work in the morning I'd never know where I'd end up at the end of the day.

For months, I worked in the Fox Casting Department grinning at a compulsive candy-eating newcomer named Diane Keaton who showed up to read for parts. I remember she was always bubbly and grateful as I handed her the dialogue to learn, all the while shoving candy corn into her mouth as fast as she could swallow. She was as thin then as she is now and the rumor in the casting department was she "…was one to watch." When we had the time, I'd run lines with her to help her memorize them. This is where I learned another invaluable lesson. You never know if dialogue works until you hear it out loud.

During the months I was assigned to the Writers Building, I'd sit across the hall from a funny, smart, inspiring man named Larry Gelbart who told me he was writing a TV pilot called M*A*S*H after Fox's movie of the same name. I was mesmerized by the way he talked, how much he had to say about story and what made a good one. He taught me that in comedy, most humor comes from the unique sadness of a situation. In M*A*S*H, the humor came from reminiscences about doctors in Korea behaving insanely to stop themselves from going insane.

He finished the M*A*S*H pilot on the last day of May and ripped off the page of his large wall calendar. Instead of throwing it away, after the word "MAY" he inscribed, "May all go well for you." and signed his name as a gift to me. I have kept it framed on my office wall ever since as inspiration. Larry Gelbart would go on to co-write the book for the hit Broadway musical A Funny Thing Happened on the Way to the Forum and the classic movie comedy Tootsie. A favorite Gelbartism of mine will always be, "One doesn't have a sense of humor. It has you."

After the Writers Building, I was sent to the Production Department where I was promoted to Production Supervisor under Unit Production Manager, Ed Haldeman. This promotion took me out of California to Santa Fe, New Mexico for my first location shoot. At twenty-two I was finally "in the movies". Thrust right out of the nest so deeply into the process, I wasn't sure I'd make it out without permanent damage.

At a motion picture studio, there is a hospital, fire and police department, twenty-four hour food and drink, a Xerox department, electricians, carpenters, wardrobe and transportation. You have support in all areas of real life as well as make believe. On the lot, a movie is made under situations that are 99% controllable. On location, it's just the opposite—you can control little or nothing. Ed Haldeman was a delicious bear of a man with a sharp wit who loved drink and a good laugh. My good luck because if I hadn't laughed, I certainly would have cried. And did, more than once as things I was responsible for seemed to systematically fall apart.

Twentieth Century Fox bought the negative to a half-finished movie they thought had box-office potential. The movie was *Billy Jack* and producer/writer/star Tom Laughlin had run out of his own money without completing the picture. Ed and I, along with assistant director, Wes McAfee, representing Fox, were to see that he stayed on budget and on schedule to finish the film whether Laughlin liked it or not.

Immediately we had one huge problem. Since finishing the first half of the movie, Tom had gained twenty pounds and had ten days to lose them before filming started again. My first job with the new lofty title of Production Supervisor was to keep him from over-eating and to buy enough Fleet Enemas to get him through those ten days. Fortunately, I did not have to insert them.

Tom was a smart man. He had opened the successful Montessori School in Santa Monica, and had a political activist's message to deliver to the world. But in spite of his intelligence, or because of it, he remained an actor with a terrible temper. Film schedules rarely bring out the best in a person and to me this was a hungry, cranky man with a huge challenge. After growing up with a father with a similar personality, I knew to give him what he wanted and tried to stay out of his way.

This was particularly tough on the days Tom arrived bright and early to give me a tape of his dreams from the night before. Another of my jobs was to type these fantasies for him. A devotee of Swiss analyst Carl Jung, Tom did not view dreams as simply describing what we did the previous day. Rather, he understood dream images and characters as energetically alive within us. Much of what Jung taught Tom about our "dream psyche" was the importance of embracing and aligning ourselves correctly with it's medicinal energies. Thus his dreams were an important guide to him for each day's work. I asked him if he minded me knowing such intimate details about him, but he just grinned and turned it around by asking, "Does it bother you to type such intimate things about me?"

The night before filming began, Tom called me at 1:00 a.m. with last-minute script changes. The production secretaries were home in their beds, and this was pre-Kinkos. This meant I had to Xerox one hundred copies before the cast and crew arrived at 5:30 a.m. Once fifty copies had been made, the machine caught fire in the hotel room we'd turned into an office. At the same time, one of the actresses, whose close-up was scheduled for early in the day, fell in her bathtub, and I had to drive her to the emergency room.

The hospital's waiting room was filled with victims of a knife fight and the actress wasn't seen until almost daylight. My fingers were numb from holding ice to her swollen temple, my mind racing for what usable angles we might have left of her face. Tom was furious that I wouldn't have time to transcribe his dreams from the night before, but he and the crew were waiting for their script changes. Neither the actress nor I had slept or eaten. That first day, filming got off to a slow and shaky start.

Later in the shoot we had a scene that called for "...people to line both sides of the road for as far as the eye could see." The local casting company failed to organize the event, so Ed Haldeman hired a flatbed truck with two thousand sandwiches and cold drinks, handed me a bullhorn and had a driver take us through town collecting people and taking them off to the set where they were stranded until Tom got his shot. The hot, dry wind was blowing sand so hard it made for a miserable day. So much for the glamour of show business.

Five long days later, on our first Sunday in New Mexico, I finally got a day off and time to sleep. When I didn't answer the phone, Tom sent his driver to get me. Led by the film's director of photography, Fred Koenekamp (*Patton*), the crew said they'd walk if he didn't let me rest. A gesture of solidarity that I will never forget.

Billy Jack became a huge hit due in large part to Laughlin's marketing strategy. Tom Laughlin ran for President three times after *Billy Jack* became a cult classic. I credit him with teaching me persistence, and to have total confidence in your projects or no one else will.

When *Hello Dolly* turned out to be a financial disaster for Twentieth Century Fox, many of us were laid off. A Fox executive and ex-marine captain named Lillian Gallo recruited me to go with her to work for Barry Diller, head of prime-time programming at ABC (and later a co-founder of the Fox network). His new concept was a weekly ninety-minute anthology series called *The Movie of the Week* and our offices hired veteran producers like Aaron Spelling and David Wolper to energize the made-for-TV movie format with fresh story concepts, fine actors and strong production values.

Our department developed and supervised a category called Movies of the Weekend including the infamous *Duel* based on a Richard Matheson short story from *Playboy*. This was twenty-four year old director Steven Spielberg's first feature film. Many of the notables I met and or worked with at ABC besides Spielberg included actors James Caan, Dennis Weaver, Robert Wagner, Natalie Wood and directors Jim Brooks (*Terms of Endearment, Broadcast News, As Good as It Gets*); Paul Wendkos, (*A Woman Called Moses, The Legend of Lizzie Borden*) and Joseph Sargent (*The Marcus Nelson Murders, Hustling*). I learned if you want to know immediately what doesn't work in your script, show it to a director. It's ultimately up to them to tell the story on film. Their notes can make or break an audience's understanding of what the writer is trying to say.

After ABC, I worked for a series of production companies that made television shows from Saturday morning series to prime time pilots and movies. I met and worked with many fine actors including Ed Asner, Jill Clayburgh, Cloris Leachman, Jonathan Winters, Burt Reynolds, Robin Williams, Larry Hagman, Diane Ladd and Melissa Gilbert. I moved from company to company gathering various experiences until ultimately landing at MGM Television as Assistant to the President, Ed Montanus.

Besides having working knowledge of every show on the MGM lot, every script, and every budget, I had my own golf cart (a huge perk even now). One of my jobs was to screen an old MGM movie a day and look for potential series ideas. In a full circle moment, as Oprah calls them, I would be living the dream.

In my early thirties, my biological clock was telling me it was time to start my own family. I married a wonderful man, financial wizard Charles Bergman, and our daughter, Sarah, was born a year later.

After our second child, Adam, arrived, I returned to writing since I could do it from home and started yet another creative run. For thirteen years without a break, the Creative Artists Agency kept me busy writing series pilots, movies for television and big-screen features. From the beginning, the scripts I sold were family oriented. I fell into a comfortable niche of being the go-to television writer for stories about strong women, most of them based in fact.

I did return to UCLA to take subsequent classes but I real-ized I already had my degree in screenwriting and production. I was lucky. I earned it from learning on the job. I had gained so much more knowledge and experience in the trenches than I would have from a classroom setting that I could begin to teach with authority. My advice? Find a style you like and emu-late it using the industry's standards I will explain in depth. Before you know it, your own distinctive voice will start telling you what to write.

I have many more stories that I will incorporate into the upcoming chapters, but now that you know everything about me, it's your turn to find out what parts of you to leave on the page.

"It must have been tough on your mother, not having any children."

—Ginger Rogers, 42nd Street (1933)

Step One.

The first step in writing that saleable script is to **find your story**.

I know. I know. You've just rolled your eyes and whispered, "Duh…" You think it's obvious because you've told me you're writing a story about a woman finding true love. The truth is I would still ask, "So, what's the story?"

There are a gazillion stories about women finding their true loves and I need to hear yours. The story that only you can write is based on your life experience, your instinct, your intuition, your research and your passion. It's your personal point of view of boy-meets-girl that makes it unique, fresh and keeps Jennifer Aniston in her $1700 a pair Manolos.

Some film stories are cradle to grave (*Ghandi*, *Fried Green Tomatoes*, *The Curious Case of Benjamin Button*), but most are just slices of that long journey. Slices are good. We like fat, juicy slices of life with surprises. You can write about yourself or someone you know or someone you read about or a character you create from scratch.

There are two ways to get started on a screenplay.
1.) Find an idea and then write characters to fit that idea. (*The Martian, The Wolf of Wall Street, Spotlight, Brooklyn*)
or
2.) Find a character first and then slide him or her into an idea. (*Forrest Gump, Dallas Buyers Club, American Sniper*)

Both approaches work. Some writers are inspired by a character, others by an incident or event. There is no right nor wrong.

Many of you already have an idea for a movie, but too many of you don't know where to start. Don't despair, for veterans and beginners, the hardest part of screenwriting is coming up with the story. Good stories have action and heart and characters that we can identify with, characters we root for. It's a big process for you to blend all of these ingredients that starts with the initial idea. So, cut yourself a little slack and try and have some fun.

So, for those who don't have an "A" story (the main thrust of your film), let's get the creative juices flowing. Below you'll find a writing exercise I offer my students in the classroom. Answer the questions listed and see whose name or what event in your life, or the life of someone you know, keeps coming up. Don't over-think your answers. (This is a game to help you explore what's lurking in your gray matter and let your idea flow.) You can't do it wrong. This is not a test!
1. Who or what inspired you to take a big chance?
2. Who or what broke your heart?
3. Who or what made you step up and do better?

4. Who or what brought you unspeakable joy?
5. Who or what changed your life for the better?
6. Who or what changed your life for the worse?
7. Who or what are you jealous of?
8. Who or what terrifies you?
9. At whom or what did you laugh the hardest?
10. What were the worst and best days of your life?

Now, write the heading "possible characters" on a clean sheet of paper. Under that, list the people who came up in your answers.

This list can be comprised of someone as important as a life partner, or as casual as the woman who works at your cleaners. Think: what characters do I know who intrigue me?

Okay, you have a list of "possible characters." Now write a new heading called "Inciting Incidents". And under that, I want you to list incidents that changed the path of your life or someone else's you know. Again, maybe it's something you read. James Franco's *127 Hours* was first a small article in a hometown newspaper, Nicole Kidman's *Rabbit Hole*, a Pulitzer Prize winning play. As the story goes, Aaron Sorkin was talking to his older sister Deborah, a Navy Judge Advocate General, about a case she had that inspired the idea that broke his career. Based on the case, he wrote a stage version of *A Few Good Men*, a military courtroom drama about Marines who killed their fellow soldier. Before the play ran, Sorkin sold the movie rights that would lead to an Oscar-nominated film starring Demi Moore in the role based on his sister. There was someone else in that film...Oh yeah, Tom Cruise. Come on, we're playing here, let your imagination run wild. No rules. No judgment. Have fun!

Look for an incident THAT TURNED A LIFE IN ANOTHER DIRECTION, even if it is a small change. It could be as big as a divorce or a death or as small as getting into the wrong car at a car wash. Come up with a list of events that could change a life's direction, e.g., meeting someone new, an accident, a trip to an exotic land, a jail sentence, a job change, going to your first AA meeting, falling off the wagon, taking a chance at something new, a divorce, a marriage, birth or death, asking for something, being asked for something, getting lost, getting found, a good haircut, a bad haircut, a pregnancy, an abortion, an epiphany of some kind, a memory.

Keep these character and incident lists and add to them. Even if you don't have an idea already, chances are your movie lies somewhere in these lists.

Another way to come up with a good idea or character is to read voraciously: novels, short stories, magazine articles, newspapers. When I first started writing screenplays, I subscribed to three small town newspapers as well as the Los Angeles and Sunday New York Times. I still keep a file of clippings of characters and places and activities that I haven't seen used on film before. You never know when that "idea file" will come in handy.

Traveling is also a good way to get your juices flowing. Seeing fresh sites, experiencing different cultures and hearing new languages often spur creativity. Have you ever been on a trip and seen the same face at the airport, then realized that person started at the same point of departure as you and ended up in the same destination? This could be a romance or a thriller depending on the story you make up about you and that other person.

Another way to find a good story is to volunteer. Drop in to a hospital, a school or a veterans organization for a month or two. These places are rife with character and story. And you can't have a movie without those two ingredients.

A tried and true way to write a good story is to revamp a classic. Aaron Sorkin says the story for *The Social Network* was inspired by Akira Kurosawa's film *Rashomon* in which a crime witnessed by four individuals is described in four mutually contradictory ways. Howard Hawk's *Red River*, which itself was inspired by Homer's *The Odyssey*, has inspired countless pictures including last year's mega blockbuster, *Avatar.*

A lot of writers check in to mythic structure for their stories to see how their ideas fall into that order. Mythic structure is the powerful relationship between mythology and storytelling that some writers use as a guideline to structure and as a source of creative inspiration. It's a popular form of structure derived from Joseph Campbell's book *The Hero With A Thousand Faces* that defines mythic structure as having the following structural elements:

Ordinary World
Call to Adventure
Refusal of the Call
Meeting the Mentor (Wise Old Man or Woman)
Crossing the First Threshold
Test, Allies, Enemies
Approach to the Inmost Cave
Supreme Ordeal
Reward (Seizing the Sword)
The Road Back
Resurrection
Return with the Elixir

Star Wars, Schindler's List, The Full Monty, Tootsie, The Wizard of Oz, The Wrestler all have mythic structure. A good adaptation of Campbell's book by Christopher Vogler specifically geared towards screenwriters is *The Writer's Journey: Mythic Structure for Writers.*

Kal Bishop, EzineArticles.com Expert Author wrote a great article the site has allowed me to use on this very subject: *Hero's Journey, Screenwriting, Story Structure – The Myth of the Flawed Hero. http://EzineArticles.com/?expert=Kal_Bishop*

> *"First," says Kal, "you have to get your head around the idea that there is really only one story. By that we mean this: every story you have ever seen or read is essentially an alternate situation superimposed, with individual style, over the same structure. The Godfather (1972), Slumdog Millionaire (2008), Brokeback Mountain (2005), Gladiator (2000), Annie Hall (1977) and every other successful story you have ever seen or read are all one and the same — various situations superimposed over the same structure. Spielberg, Lucas, Scorsese, Coppola, Cameron all use this structure. Shakespeare used this structure. Stories in the Bible, the Vedas, the Torah and the Koran use this structure. You can use this structure.*
>
> *The Hero's Journey is the template upon which the majority of successful screenplays are built. Films as diverse as The Martian (2015), Gladiator (2000), Million Dollar Baby (2004), Raging Bull (1980) and Scarface (1983) were all constructed around the Hero's Journey pattern (also known as the Monomyth).*
>
> *There is an argument that the flawed hero is the perfect hero. To make the hero three dimensional, human ailments and weaknesses must be present, but it all depends on your story. There are various types of hero: a) the good, willing hero (Star Wars, 1977), b) the good, unwilling hero (Shawshank Redemption, 1994), c) the anti-hero (Raging Bull, 1980), d) the villain (Goodfellas, 1990). All are simply some of the possible hero archetypes: you choose which one is relevant for you."*

The key to writing your own mini mythic story is to go
back to the lists you created from the exercise above and think
of a time in your life when you had conflict or went through a
big change. Look back to see when you got into trouble, or you
had to face something challenging, or life threw you a curve
ball. I'm sure you have more than one of these incidents on
which you could base an "A" story.

A PROTAGONIST (the guy, gal or concept we are rooting
for) is the central character in a screenplay. An ANTAGONIST
(the bad guy, the villain, the big obstacle) is a character who is
opposite to or challenges the protagonist. You must give your
protagonist needs and goals and then create obstacles to him or
her achieving those goals. Without these conflicts you have no
action, and without action you have no movie.

Think of the plot or story as a rollercoaster and the characters as the passengers on that rollercoaster. What decisions do
they have to make, what steps do they have to take, what do
they have to hide, how far out of their comfort zone do they
have to go, to make it back to the ride's terminal – or not?

Story material can come when you least expect it. I once
told a brunch mate, Martin Tahse, that I had gone to Alateen
because of my parents' alcohol abuse. Voila. A saleable story to
a major network.

And there was the time I was sitting with a student, Lila
Silvern, who wrote many hilarious stand-up comedy routines
for seniors. We had become dear friends over the course of
a few years. I was heartbroken to learn her beloved first son,
a newspaper journalist, had died of a brain tumor. Before he
died, he insisted she freeze his sperm. When she ran some new
comedy material past me on what to do with the sperm, I was
stunned at how brave she was, how funny and gut-wrenching
the material was and how absolutely, positively it had to be a

movie! She is currently working with me to find the story and it will be her first screenplay.

Characters and inciting incidents are all around you. You just have to train your mind to watch and listen as a **screenwriter** and you'll find them.

I always demand my students read as many good scripts as they can get their hands on. You can download for free at www.SimplyScripts.com or www.scripts-onscreen.com and watch the films of those scripts. The more you read, the more elements you'll recognize as necessary for a film. I promise you will start to recognize "A" stories or interesting characters as they come your way.

Please, don't try to figure out Hollywood's latest hot topics. By the time you catch on to them they will be cold. Invest in your best personal story, the one you are most passionate about and make the characters relatable and sympathetic. Richard Walter, head of UCLA's screenwriting program, says "There are only two kinds of scripts, good and bad."

I like to think of it another way. There are two kinds of scripts, one that follows the industry-accepted rules, and one that doesn't. Which brings me to:

YOUR LOGLINE — THE COIN OF THE REALM

Okay. You found your great idea and you're ready to sit down and write it overnight, sell it for millions and buy that private jet. You see yourself pouring champagne as all of your friends on board toast your success. Great! But before you type a word of your screenplay, there is one ESSENTIAL thing you must KNOW; one thing you must BELIEVE IN and REMAIN TRUE TO; and, one thing you must KNOW BY HEART. "What is it?" you ask, tapping your chin thoughtfully. What is it? Indeed!

The first question any agent/buyer/publisher/reader/executive/actor will ask about your project is "What is it?" or "What's it about?" or "What's the logline?"

The LOGLINE is your most valuable tool for selling your project, and you must know what it is before you start to write your script. Unless, of course, you already have a perfectly fleshed-out story with a beginning, middle and ironic end. Do you? If so, then write the logline for your story (BEFORE YOU START THE SCRIPT!) and proceed to match your logline to the script.

I owe thanks to my phenomenal teachers—the Godfather of Screenplay, Syd Field, and the ingenious beat-sheet king, Blake Snyder—who taught me that the logline is make or break time. In my classroom, logline day is the most hateful day of all. Many call it the logline from hell day. Why? Because loglines are hard to write, hard to nail, and I won't let up on my students until they nail it.

<u>The logline is the hero's story.</u> IT'S WHERE YOU START!

In my opinion, and the opinion of many others, you cannot write a successful script unless you first come up with a concise, ironic and provocative sentence that reflects exactly what you want your movie to be. Then, and only then, can you deliver that same story in your script. That doesn't mean if a story is leaking out of your pores, you shouldn't write it down. It means, after it's on paper in straight storytelling mode, see if you can write an intriguing, clever logline from what you wrote. If you can't, then the story has problems.

Let me say it another way. If you can't make your logline work — maybe you're trying to write a story that doesn't work. Hello? Before you invest hours of time in something that doesn't work, create a logline that solves the problems and rewrite the story to match. **Yes, change the story to match the logline!**

Nailing it down and sticking to it is vital to your story as you beat it out. It makes you examine who your hero is, who the bad guy/situation is and what scenes/info you need to fill out your 100 plus pages of screenplay. When you are clear where you are going, there is very little guesswork left. The LOGLINE IS A TOOL TO HELP YOU STICK TO YOUR STORY.

So, let's get remedial. What is a logline or a "one liner" as some people call it?

A logline is one sentence that tells the world what your movie is about. It answers the question "What is it?" Sometimes, it's a run-on sentence. But it's one sentence that will open doors or close them.

Long before anyone reads your script, this one sentence will be read or said about 150 times.

Most pros don't read past the logline, so you have to grab them quickly. I've read that the logline is the coin of the realm in Hollywood. So, if you want to make big bucks writing screenplays, you've got to start with the coins first.

Writing something short and exciting is never easy. It takes practice. Read and study professionally written loglines in newspapers, magazines, Variety, and Internet film reviews. Google "good loglines"! Find examples of what will help you express your story concept in one sentence.

A good logline should clearly answer these FOUR QUESTIONS:

- Who is your main character?
- What does he or she want?
- Who is trying to stop him or her?
- What happens if he or she fails?

These four questions will keep you focused as a writer.

Remember that the logline needs to create a strong, emotional, ironic pitch that draws a compelling mental picture and gets your script into the movie theater or onto TV. Yikes! It seems impossible to do all of that in one sentence, but read on.

The logline works if the words chosen reveal the story's marketability by genre (comedy, drama, thriller), tone (funny, sad, scary) emotional pull (relatable), audience (who will want to see this?) and cost. Want to see some examples?

How about this from my new script, *Not Dead Yet:* To cross over, a newly dead young woman must lead her grieving fiancé to the woman he *should* marry causing havoc on the set of his reality show.

What do the buyers know from this one run-on sentence? They know it's not expensive. How? It's a reality show that the ghost crashes, so everyone just has to be attractive but not necessarily a star.   It's sure to be filmed in primarily one location. (My money's on a hideously decorated Malibu mansion.) Reality means sex. Newly dead means fantasy. Grieving ex-fiancé means love and tears. Buyers know exactly who their audience is: Women! Everything is clear in one sentence. The writer hears the magic phrase, "Send it over."

Here's another great example: *4 Christmases:* A newly married couple must spend Christmas Day with all four of their divorced parents.

Again, we know it's not expensive. You've got twenty-somethings and stunt casting for the parents: DeNiro, Dustin Hoffman, Barbra Streisand. (Stunt casting means a big star in a supporting role, not the lead.)

And from a good logline you can zero in on a killer title. *4 Christmases* could have been called *Christmas Crazed* or *Too Many Mangers,* but those titles don't pinpoint what it is.

4 *Christmases* tells us what it is. If your logline and title don't pass the "what it is" test, keep writing.

Here's the structure of a good logline:

ADJECTIVE [protagonist] [verb] [antagonist] [goal] [stakes].

Many say THE ADJECTIVE is optional, but I feel it is hugely important to create irony. It must describe your lead efficiently, e.g., harried, naive, nasty, cranky, flighty, grieving, serious, no-nonsense, cheap, incensed, alcoholic.

THE VERB you choose to depict the struggle must be visual, impacting and active. Best to use a verb that suits the genre, with or without an auxiliary verb (must, have to, will), and indicates necessity, e.g., (must) deliver, struggle, (has to) battle, fight, contend, wrestle, take on, win, joust, duel, destroy, spar, scrap, oppose etc.

Keep rewriting until it excites you. Then try it out on friends. See if they react with interest. See if they get it. When they do, you know you've got it. As formulistic as all this sounds, expect to rewrite your logline many, many times as you develop your story and script.

When you're working out the story, the logline might change. This is good, as long as the logline works. When you read the examples below this will be much clearer, and you will see it is not as complicated as it sounds. Note the irony in all.

— A shy Irish immigrant in 1950s New York falls for a tough Italian, but faces temptation from a local man when she returns to Ireland for a visit. *Brooklyn*

— Left behind by his crew, an astronaut must learn to survive on Mars and find a way to contact Earth. *The Martian*

— An unemotional businessman falls in love with a hook-
er he hires for the weekend. *Pretty Woman*

— After an unscheduled landing, an efficiency expert is
stranded on a deserted island and must survive against all
odds. *Cast Away*

— A mild-mannered, detached father must learn to
reconnect with his two nasty daughters after his wife dies. *The
Descendants*

—A door mat youngest daughter of a dysfunctional Italian
family rises to become founder and matriarch of a powerful
business dynasty. *Joy*

Again, let me impress upon you the importance of the
logline in the entertainment business. The logline with the
most conflict, the most sharply defined hero and bad guy, and
the clearest, most primal goal, is the winner. DON'T LEAVE
HOME WITHOUT IT.

Once you've made your creative decisions, write the story
out in treatment form for yourself. A treatment is a detailed
summary of the plot, 20-45 pages long. It includes brief
descriptions of your characters as they first appear. It can also
include some scene descriptions and random dialogue. In it
you tell your story as if you were telling it to a friend, as if it
were happening at the moment. Tell what happened sequentially, trimmed to the essentials. Remember to establish your
characters' desires, needs and goals, then what keeps him or
her from them. The best way to do it is let your story flow without paying too much attention to structure, and then in the
next pass (the next rewrite), start sharpening your focus.

If you're still having difficulty finding your best story, look
for the story arc. A story arc is one sentence that connects the
beginning to the end. How can that be simpler? I know what
you're thinking. "Well, if I don't know what my story is, how
in the heck do I know its arc?"

Aha. Even simpler. To find the story arc, ask yourself, "What does my protagonist want at the beginning and what happens at the end?" This thread becomes your "A" story or the spine of your movie (also called the backbone, the core thread, the through-line, the primary story). You have to know your "A" story before you can create your subplots.

Still stuck? Let's go back to the list of characters you made earlier. Take a look at the names of possible characters. Next to each name, answer the question, "What does he or she want?" Don't over think this for the exercise. Make it up if you need to. Make it real, make it loony, make it scary. All that matters is that for this exercise, you come up with something effortlessly. Then ask, "What happened at the end?" You can have more than one conclusion at this point. In fact, you'll probably have a bunch.

In *The King's Speech*, what did Bertie want? He wanted to speak without stuttering. What happened at the end? He kept his country's morale high as he led them through WWII using only his voice on the radio.

In *Room* what did Ma want? She wanted to give her son a full, albeit make-believe, world in captivity. What happened at the end? They escaped and she now has to redefine what is real in the world.

In *Casablanca*, what did Rick want? He wanted to live out the war without involvement or hassle. What happened at the end? He put his freedom at risk to save his long lost love, Ilse, and her spy husband.

Note the irony here, screenwriters!

I heard Aaron Sorkin explain how he wrote the first and last scenes of *"The Social Network."* Sorkin says he had access to Zuckerberg's blog post from the night he was dumped by his girlfriend and hacked into Harvard's computer system to create "Facemash." Sorkin said, "...and I wanted to see the scene that caused him to write that...once I knew how it was going to open, I knew what the end was."

This speaks to the importance of knowing your ending before you begin your screenplay. If you don't know your ending, the tendency is to write yourself into a corner because you get lost. If you know where you are going, you can point all scenes in that direction and stay on course. More on this in the next chapter.

What did *Juno* want? She wanted to find perfect parents to adopt her baby. That's it. And what happened at the end? She gave the baby to the mother to raise by herself because the husband bolted. That's the arc of the movie. It is the "A" story, the spine. Juno wanted a set of perfect parents to adopt her baby... and in the end, she got one instead. Diablo Cody's first screenplay is an Academy Award winner. This is as simple as a story can be.

Remember the rollercoaster. Your job is to take the characters along with the readers for a great ride all the way to the end. You must know your end before you start.

Now that you know your story and have the perfect logline, let's move onto screenplay structure.

"Have fun storming the castle!"

—Miracle Max, *The Princess Bride* (1987)

Step Two.

Shape Your Story. Find its beginning, middle and end, plot points and midpoint.

Good work! You've done your writing exercises, made your lists of possible inciting incidents, thought a lot about characters, researched the story you want to write about and put it in treatment form. Now it's time to shape it into a screenplay. But first, let's get go back to the basics.

What is a screenplay? A screenplay is a written plan for a film. It is a story told with moving pictures (scenes) strung together with dialogue and description. It has a beginning called Act I, a middle called Act II and an end called Act III. The scenes or units of action in each act build to a climax or conclusion at the end of Act III. This is where your main character solves the problem you set up for him in Act I, or not. It is even more simply, a road map for the cast and crew so that everyone on the set knows what his or her job is on any given day. All departments from props, wardrobe, electrics, transportation to set decorators, even the camera crew, take their cues from your script and its structure.

What is structure? It's simply the arrangement of the units of action we call scenes to build to a final conflict and resolution. The root of the word structure, struct, means to build. The three-act paradigm or pattern (see example pictured on page 53) is often attributed to Syd Field who applied Aristotle's Poetics to screenwriting. Aristotle said a properly formed plot must have a beginning, which is not a necessary consequence of any previous action; a middle, which follows logically from the beginning; and an end, which follows logically from the middle and from which no further action necessarily follows.

And here's the good news: whether you're writing a romantic comedy, a suspense thriller, a historical drama or big budget science fiction, all successful Hollywood movies follow the same basic three-act structure. Unless you're related to producer Harvey Weinstein (*Carol, Silver Linings Playbook, Shakespeare in Love*) and he owes you, or you've sold a dozen scripts, learn this structure and stick to it.

One of the best things I learned over the years is to know my script ending before I start. It's your ultimate destination and if you lose focus on it, the script will lose focus and that is the ruination of any possible sale. Don't just meander along in search of an ending. Know it going in. By ending, I mean resolution. How does the story wrap up? What happens? Did the protagonist get what he or she wanted? You need to find this out when you're searching for your story, not when you're about to start the screenplay.

Listen, along the way, you may find a better ending. It could creep up on you in the shower or while walking the dog, and that's a gift you'll accept graciously. But it should come as your well thought-out choice, not as a quickie fixer-upper because you've let the plot fly out of control. Know your ending and work up to it in the time parameters of a film whether it be funny, sad or downright tragic. In television, that's 90 plus minutes. In film, 100-120 minutes.

For purposes of instruction in this book, let's say all screenplays are 100 pages. In breaking up your three divisions of story telling, your first act should be one fourth of that or 25 pages. Act II, your second division of the story, is twice that or 50 pages. Act III comes in at one fourth and another 25 pages. In the screenplay three-act paradigm, you need to know seven things:

1. The opening. These days no professional will read past page ten if he or she is not "hooked" on your style or idea. Make the first ten pages pop! Write SCENES THAT ARE FRESH AND UNUSUAL, scenes that compel the reader to keep turning the pages.

2. The plot point near the end of Act I (on or about page 23) signaling the story's overt move in another direction. A plot point, sometimes called a reversal, is a game changing scene that hooks into the story and thrusts it in a new and eye-opening direction, leading into the next act of the screenplay.

3. The end of Act I (on or about page 25).

4. The literal midpoint (on or about page 50) where an event so shakes the character, he or she can no longer turn back but must fully take on the problem.

5. The plot point near the end of Act II (on or about page 73) spinning us into Act III.

6. The end of Act II (on or about page 75).

7. The resolution at the end of Act III and the aftermath (on or about page 100).

You'll learn that each of these seven markers on the paradigm affects the others. As writer-director Billy Wilder (*Some Like It Hot*) famously said, "If you have a problem with the third act, you have a problem in the first act."

There is a lot of controversy about whether to structure or not and what method to use. There are as many methods and variations of methods to get to the perfect structure as there are boy-meets-girl stories, but one thing pretty much remains the same: **A saleable screenplay has a classic three-act structure.** Even movies for television start with that same structure, and are then modified to fit each network's schedule of commercial breaks.

For me, there is no controversy. In writing a screenplay, structure is everything. You must have a formula when starting out. When you give your screenplay to a producer or an agent, he or she will give it to a "reader" first to provide a short summary of the story and a recommendation. The way it works is that you'll get a "yes" or a "no" right away from a complete stranger.

Before reading a word, this professional will thumb through your masterpiece to see if you have a structure in place, an acceptable page count, decent dialogue and crisp, economical descriptions. If not, it will get tossed into the return pile or the round file, unless your sister is married to the head of the studio. Then it probably will be read no matter how badly you put it together. Before we get into the nuts and bolts of structure, here are a few overall thoughts you must commit to if you want to be taken seriously as a screenwriter.

Screenplays are shorter than they used to be. 100 to 115 pages is the norm. When I worked at ABC's Movies of the

Weekend, executive Lillian Gallo would literally pick the lightest weight script for her weekend reading. That rule still holds true today. Unless you're a name writer with a bunch of Oscars displayed in your bathroom, the first measure of whether or not your newborn is saleable is its weight and length. If it feels too heavy, it goes to the bottom of the stack. Start learning to write cleverly and economically right away.

You must use an accepted industry format. I always recommend Final Draft. Buy it, and learn how to use it before you begin to input your script. Even though it is user-friendly, there can be a learning curve and you don't want to add additional stress to the already anxious process of writing your first draft.

A screenplay takes place in the moment so it must be written in present tense no matter how many years ago it happened or how many years in the future it might happen. The character smokes in the darkened alley, not the character is smoking. As Ram Dass said, "Be here now."

No new important characters should be introduced after Act I. Act I is the beginning and all stories start there. No exceptions. We don't have to literally see all characters in Act I, but they need to be mentioned or "set up" as part of the story. This is where you apply your most clever self. Find a way to weave in the characters early even if it's as simple as showing a photo of the killer on a police station bulletin board as in *Witness*. Having the young boy recognize a cop in a photograph tacked to a bulletin board on the police station wall was a stunning and clever introduction of the antagonist. We learned the bad guy was a cop and the drama was upped immediately.

In Robert Towne's *Chinatown*, Jack Nicholson's character "Gittes" meets a Mrs. Mulwray who hires him to prove her husband, Mr. Mulwray, is cheating. It turns out she was an imposter, but for story purposes, we did meet a Mrs. Mulwray in Act I. The fact that someone was impersonating her adds to the richness of the mystery right out of the gate.

Do not have any new characters jumping out at your reader after Act I. This is the sign of an amateur who doesn't know the three act structure.

Let's get our acts together, shall we?

ACT I

Back in the day when Aristotle was crafting his Poetics, he declared Act I The Beginning. But we can do better than that. We can call Act I the set up, the trail head, the kick off, the platform, the status quo, the way things are for your characters — physically and mentally—as they jump off into the story. It is the hook, the introduction, the orientation to this juicy slice of life we are creating. Act I is the way the characters look and feel when they first step into the rollercoaster car before their hair gets blown into a bird's nest and their eyes tear. Act I is the first division of your three-act structure and it has a demanding job. It:

1. introduces your characters.
2. sets up the protagonist's goals and problems.
3. contains the first plot point (on or about page 23).
4. introduces the OR ELSE factor (what the hero has at risk).

Syd Field calls it the OR ELSE factor, but it is simply what your hero puts at risk if he or she doesn't get what they want. Mainly it is what fate has in store for your characters if they don't solve the problem. The OR ELSE factor ups the tension and charges your piece with needed suspense, even in love stories.

In *Concussion*, Will Smith's character either proves that football causes irrevocable brain damage OR ELSE loses all credibility.

In *The Revenant*, Leonardo Di Caprio either keeps the fires of revenge burning to spur him forward, OR ELSE he'll die.

In *Birdman*, Michael Keaton's desperate Broadway produc-er/actor/writer either makes his play a success OR ELSE admits he's a failure.

In *Brooklyn*, the Irish immigrant, Eilis, has to find a future in America OR ELSE go home to her village where there is little work nor hope.

In *127 Hours*, Aron Ralston either frees his arm OR ELSE he dies in Blue John Canyon, Utah.

Let's recap. In Act I, we've met our hero and antagonists, we've created needs and goals, set up our OR ELSE factor. Remember, the "A" story is the main through-line of the movie. It is what the protagonist wants. Now we're ready for our protagonist's first plot point on or about page 23. Time to ruffle your readers' undies and spin the story in another direction into Act II.

WHAT IS A PLOT POINT? In the three-act structure, all scenes are plot points but two of them are more significant than the rest, and you need to make them so. PP1 (plot point one) and PP2 (plot point two) are story changers and help keep you headed in the right (saleable) direction.

A plot point in the three-act structure is a scene that grabs our attention because it alters the story in a significant way and often changes its course. Think of it as a fractured connector bar on the rollercoaster car that causes it to break away from the rest, careen off the side, and shake up the passengers before falling back onto the track below. It's still flying down the tracks but faster and on a different course.

Or think of a plot point as a huge bolder that falls into a creek and forces the water to flow through a smaller opening thus creating rapids, debris and a stronger thrust. The charac-ters, like the creek, have to adapt to continue to flow. What will your characters do to adapt?

In *The Hurt Locker*, PP1 comes on a first outing with a new team, the hot shot Lt. James tosses a smoke bomb in the street effectively making himself invisible and putting all of their lives in danger. After he has revealed himself as this loose cannon, his squad sees him and treats him differently sending the story down a different path.

In *Juno*, PP1 (page 20) turns the story in another direction when Juno realizes that because she's a kid in high school with no means of support, she can't handle an abortion. Now what?

In *True Grit*, PP1 changes the story direction when, on page 29, Le Beouf forces his way into Mattie's tracking party.

In *The King's Speech*, PP1 comes on page 25 when Bertie fights with Lionel Logue about Logue's impertinence, then storms out.

Finding Plot Point One is an important step. You want something big to happen, but remember to stay within your genre (type of film) and what makes sense in the realm of your story's possibilities. You don't want to be writing a love story and then have the lover turn into a homicidal maniac from a "slasher" film. Nor do you want the tough guy in a crime story to end up in a teary, sissy heap when his wife gets killed. Plot points must be big but believable, unless, of course, you're writing fantasy.

ACT II

No matter what language you speak, the answer to "Where's the beef?" is in Act II. It's the heart, the soul, and the body of your script and twice as long as the set up or beginning. In Act II, our hero battles the obstacles from the rollercoaster car to achieve his or her desires, parrying and thrusting himself into the point of no return. At this point, he has no choice but to fully commit to solving the problem. Act II is the home for our continued subplots (stories created by our supporting characters) and Plot Point Two which raises the stakes even higher and careens us yet again even more wildly around the track to the conclusion or Act III.

In Act II we find another important structural marker, the literal **MIDPOINT** on page 50. Remember, we're using a 100 page script as our prototype. Sparks fly and there is a loud thud as the runaway car hangs over the side again, this time from one wheel. This event causes us to catch our breath because it so deeply resonates our hero's failure and impending doom. There is no way he could turn back even if he could. He must commit to do whatever it takes to continue the journey. It is your clever writing that decides what that will be.

In a typical arc, the highest point is the middle. That's how your story flows. Everything in the first half builds up to the midpoint realization, and then it all tumbles down towards the climax. The midpoint is either a really good moment or a really bad one. It will either be a false peak or a false collapse.

Blake Snyder, the brilliant author of *Save The Cat* says, "There are two halves in a movie script and the midpoint is the threshold between them." He discovered, and I have found in reviewing hundreds of good movie scripts, that a movie's midpoint is either an "UP" where the hero seemingly gets it all (but it is a false peak) or a "DOWN" where his world collapses (but it is a false collapse because our hero has some lessons to learn before we end the story). You can go either way. Make your midpoint a down or an up. This is how screenwriters create the DRAMA needed to keep the readers and later, the filmgoers, interested. You hear the stakes are raised at the midpoint, because they are.

To make the importance of the midpoint clearer to you, let's continue looking at the Academy Award nominated, *Brooklyn*. It's the story of Eilis, an Irish immigrant girl, looking for her future in America. In Act I she says goodbye to her depressed mother, her evil part-time boss and her beloved sister, Rose, to board a ship for America. Rose has arranged sponsorship for Eilis with a Catholic priest in Brooklyn where she is given a room in a boarding house and a job at a department store.

Although she tries to fit in at work and at home she can't because of paralyzing homesickness. At PP1. she collapses in tears unable to do her job. In a bold move, the good father enrolls her in business school, thrusting her into a new environment altogether and changing the course of the story into Act II.

In Act II, Eilis, our heroine, battles the obstacles to achieve his or her goal or *must-have*. Eilis' must-have is a future. So, at the midpoint, she has no choice but to fully commit to solving the problem. At the midpoint, Eilis must commit to finding a future.

She has spent the entire first half of the script trying to be American and fit in. She meets Tony, her love interest, at a dance. He expresses his love and talks of their future – all that Eilis has wanted. But then, at the midpoint, her sister Rose dies suddenly, and Eilis must return to Ireland. She is thrust into doubt about where her home actually is. Devastating, right? But it's a false down because, in the second half, she learns everything she needs to learn in Ireland to erase all doubt regarding her future, and she ends up back in America with her husband, Tony.

While we're at it, let's look at some other midpoints.

In *Juno*, the midpoint comes on pages 50-51 when Juno defies logic and the law and drives out unannounced to show the parents-to-be the ultrasound picture of their baby. What she learns is the perfect Dad isn't interested in having the baby at all – and her bubble is burst. This is a "down" choice. We are led to believe this is the worst thing that can happen. And yet, it's a false down because at the end, it turns out, his wife divorces him and becomes the perfect loving parent.

In *The Descendants*, the midpoint comes on page 47 when George Clooney's character decides to find his wife's lover and tell him she's got just a few days to live, and if he wants to say goodbye, he should have that opportunity. Even a rat should have a chance to say goodbye. This too is a false down. A false down because finding the rat and telling him he knows about the affair is the most liberating thing George's character gets to do in the entire movie. It releases him from his pain and allows him to let go of his dying wife and reconnect with his kids.

After the midpoint, Act II reveals our second plot point. This needs to be an even more devastating event or shakeup that builds and spins the story into the resolution or Act III.

PP2, placed just before the end of Act II raises the stakes even more. Perhaps a bullet between the eyes, if your name is action director John Woo. (*Face/ Off*, *Windwalkers*) This second plot point has the audience watching more intently as the whole rollercoaster car hangs from the track.

In *True Grit*, PP2 comes on page 85 and ratchets up tension when Rooster quits Mattie's hunting party leaving her with the abuser, Le Beouf.

In *Birdman*, PP2 comes when the critic in the bar tells Riggan she is going to kill his play without even seeing it.

In *The Help*, PP2 comes when Minnie threatens to pull her stories from Skeeter's book unless she tells the real story about the poop in the pie. She feels the truth is the only defense from getting found out and killed.

As far as the three act structure goes, remember that PP2 is the scene that catapults us into the finale or the resolution of our story.

In *The Fighter*, PP2 hits on page 85 when Mickey breaks his hand for the third time. Will he ever fight again?

ACT III

In Act III, all crises flare their brightest. Our hero either overcomes the problems or succumbs to them. Do or die. He remains in the rollercoaster car and arrives safely back at the station – or not. All action in this act leads to the resolution of the problems. This is the hour of truth, your turning point to the climax of the picture, and its aftermath. Act III is about 25 pages or 1/4 of your script.

In *Little Miss Sunshine*, the obstacles continue for little Olive and her family in Act III, building to a conclusion. They get to the pageant with just a minute to spare before the contest is to start. The woman in charge won't let them enroll Olive because they are late. They finagle their way in only to realize she doesn't have the right costumes or hair, or body or face. Conclusion? The family realizes how shallow the whole contest is and value what they mean to each other. The aftermath? They celebrate Olive's losing the contest. The family is happy once again.

In *The Social Network,* the story ends with Zuckerberg agreeing to settle lawsuits against him. The aftermath? He is still without the girlfriend who he hoped to regain with his success.

In *Joy*, Jennifer Lawrence's character has built a number of successful businesses for her entire dysfunctional family to work and prosper.

In *Moneyball*, Billy will return as the Athletics General Manager along with Peter. His daughter is happy her dad is staying in town.

In *Carol*, Theresa finally forgives Carol for leaving her and agrees to try again.

As I mentioned earlier, this three act formula applies to all scripts – thrillers, comedies, romance, bios, slice of life dramas. Just make sure to set the tone or style of your piece right away and don't veer from it. If it's a comedy, start immediately with a funny image. If it's a horror film, get to fear quickly. If it's a romance, let it be light and airy. If you use the formula, it will work for you.

In film, the rule is one minute of screen time per typed page. In the theatre, Act IIIs feel even shorter because they are edited more quickly to climax. Please look at my expanded adaptation of Syd Field's Three Act Screenplay Structure paradigm that I use in my classroom. This one is specific to the script of Brooklyn.

SYD FIELD THREE ACT SCREENPLAY PARADIGM
(Including Blake Snyder's All is Lost Moment)
"BROOKLYN" 108 page script

ACT I	ACT II	ACT III	
(Beginning or Set Up)	(Middle or confrontation)	(Resolution)	
Approx. pages 1-24=¼ script	Approx. pages 25-78=½ script	Pages 79-108=¼ script	ENDING
A. Introduce your protagonist, antagonist, key characters	Intensify problems, add obstacles	All is lost moment.	Eilis returns to Tony.
B. Face him with problem or crises.	First Part / Second Part	Eilis doesn't know where home is.	
C. Set up what needs to be fixed. Add the OR ELSE FACTOR.	At MIDPOINT pg 54 Hero must take on problem.	Ireland? America?	
(The dreadful alternative) Eilis must find a future or else stay impoverished in Ireland.	Eilis' beloved sister dies. Eilis wonders why she ever left Ireland.		

Plot Point 1 occurs
pg 24 Eilis collapses at work.
Propels story into ACT Two.

Plot Point 2 occurs
Pg 71 Eilis' mother insists she
return to Ireland. Propels story
to resolution.

AS YOU WRITE YOUR TREATMENT you must discover 6 things: BEGINNING, PLOT POINT 1, the MIDPOINT, PLOT POINT 2, the ALL IS LOST MOMENT, and ENDING.

EVERYBODY'S BEATING THE CAT!

You can't read any blog or visit any screenwriting site these days without hearing mention of Blake Snyder's *Save The Cat Beat Sheet*. Everyone is talking about it, explaining and using the sheet to breakdown movies into their structure. And it's all for a good reason. The Beat Sheet is an amazing tool for organizing your story! I highly recommend you use it in addition to Syd Field's paradigm.

Below you will find my breakdown of the movie *Brooklyn* using the Snyder beat sheet. The parts in **bold** are the explanations of Snyder's 15 beats. The pg. numbers in your screenplay should come on or about the page numbers he shows. MY BREAKDOWN IS IN CAPS.

BEAT 1. Opening Image (pg. 1): The audience is first engaged with something compelling that sets the tone & mood – and we begin to see things as they are right now (they will be clearly different at the end).
RESIDENTIAL STREET IN IRELAND, 1950'S – PREDAWN EILIS (PRONOUNCED ALISH), 22, SLIPS OUT OF A DREARY ROW HOUSE INTO THE DARK, RAINY MORNING. THERE IS NO ONE IN SIGHT AS SHE WALKS QUICKLY TO CHURCH.

2. Theme Stated (pg 4.): Usually spoken to the main character in a snippet of dialogue, this gives a sense of the deeper issues that this story is "about".
WE LEARN HER BELOVED SISTER ROSE HAS ARRANGED A SPONSORSHIP TO AMERICA WITH A PRIEST IN

BROOKLYN THAT INCLUDES HOUSING AND A JOB. AS
SHE PACKS EILIS' SUITCASE, ROSE TELLS HER SHE'D BUY
EILIS ANYTHING SHE WANTS BUT SHE CANNOT BUY
HER A FUTURE. THEME: YOU HAVE TO FIND YOUR OWN
FUTURE.

3. Set-Up Section (pgs.1-10): We meet the main character,
who's living a compromised life in some way, while dealing
with problems. WE NEED TO CARE ABOUT THEIR
JOURNEY. This is where you grab or lose your audience.
We get a broad enough sense of their "status quo" life to
feel we know that things MUST CHANGE. We see the
world through their eyes, and will for the rest of the movie
— Every character in the A story is introduced or made
reference to. WE should know by now what needs fixing in
the hero's life.
WE MEET EILIS' NASTY PART-TIME BOSS, THEN HER
DEPRESSED MOTHER, AND UNDERSTAND THE SMALL
MINDEDNESS OF THE COMMUNITY. THERE IS NO REAL
WORK NOR LIFE IN THE OFFING FOR EILIS. HER BEST
FRIEND, NANCY, IS INTERESTED IN ONE OF THE ELIGI-
BLE BACHELORS, BUT EILIS THINKS ALL THE RUGBY
MEN ARE SILLY. THE LOVE BETWEEN THE SISTERS IS PAL-
PABLE AND THEIR PARTING, BITTERSWEET.

4. Catalyst (pg. 12): An event rocks the main character's
world completely, and sets in motion the central problem
of the story. It's an external problem (not just internal,
about thoughts and emotions) that demands to be dealt
with now – it has clear and present stakes we can identify
with and feel.
THE VOYAGE IS A NIGHTMARE. EILIS MEETS HER CABIN
MATE, THE EXPERIENCED GEORGINA, WHO HELPS HER

SURVIVE THE ROUGH CROSSING, THE HOMESICKNESS, AND THE FEAR OF THE UNKNOWN. SHE GIVES EILIS A MAKEOVER AND TEACHES HER HOW TO ACT "AMERI-CAN" TO PASS IMMIGRATION OFFICIALS.

5. Debate <u>Section</u> (pgs. 12-25): The main character ques-tions what has happened, tries to figure out what to do, and often seeks to avoid the true "call to adventure." But they don't just talk: they take initial logical actions to try to fix things, which fail, narrowing their options.
EILIS LIVES ONLY FOR LETTERS FROM IRELAND. SHE'S TERRIBLY HOMESICK, ANXIOUS, UNCOMFORTABLE AND LOST AT WORK AND AT THE BOARDING HOUSE. SHE'S TOO HOMESICK TO EVEN TRY TO FIT IN.

6. Break into Act Two (pg. 25): The main character enters an "upside down world" – where they're completely out of their element. This is a new arena for them, where they're overmatched as they attempt to confront their story prob-lem. (They will stay in this "antithesis" to their normal life until the Break into Three.)
WHEN EILIS COLLAPSES IN TEARS AT WORK, HER SPON-SOR, FATHER FLOOD, TELLS HER SHE CAN'T GIVE UP BECAUSE THERE IS NOTHING IN IRELAND FOR HER. IN A BOLD MOVE, HE ENROLLS HER IN BOOKKEEPING SCHOOL.

7. B Story (pg. 30): A second story begins, which will run parallel to the "A Story", and interweave with it through-out the rest of the movie. The theme and the character's inner journey tends to be explored here. (Often it's the "love story," or deals with some relationship issue. Like the "A Story," it's about a <u>problem</u> that builds and

develops. It can't be a relationship that's going well.)
(B STORY)
BOOKEEPING SCHOOL IS HARD. SHE JUGGLES STUDY-
ING AND WORK WITH VOLUNTEERING TO HELP FATHER
FLOOD WITH THE POOR IRISH MEN IN HIS PARISH.
THEIR MUSIC UNDERSCORES HER HOMESICKNESS, AND
THE HARSH REALITY OF BEING AN IMMIGRANT SINKS
IN. SHE IS TORN BETWEEN BEING IRISH AND WANTING
TO BE AN AMERICAN. AT A DANCE, SHE MEETS TONY, A
CHARMING ITALIAN PLUMBER. HE IS IMMEDIATELY
SMITTEN. SHE LETS HIM ESCORT HER HOME.

8. Fun and Games Section (pgs. 30-55:The entertaining
aspects of the story's premise are explored (in scenes that
might make the movie trailer) – highlighting the main character's discomfort with this "upside down world"– which
are fun to watch, but NOT fun for the main character, who
is essentially in HELL until the end of the story, when the
problem becomes more focused, more serious, more impor-
tant and urgent.
EILIS IS STILL HOME SICK. TONY BEGINS SHOWING UP
TO WALK HER HOME FROM SCHOOL. WHEN HE'S LATE
ONE NIGHT, SHE BECOMES CONCERNED, MISSING HIM.
TONY ADMITS HIS LOVE FOR HER. SHE GRADUATES
FROM SCHOOL. SHE LOOKS FOR WORK. TONY TAKES
HER TO CONEY ISLAND AND TEACHES HER TO WEAR
HER BATHING SUIT UNDER HER CLOTHES. SHE WRITES
HOME THAT SHE IS HAPPY FOR THE FIRST TIME SINCE
LEAVING IRELAND.

9. Midpoint. (pg. 54 in B) This is the threshold between
the two halves of your story. This is where the hero fully
takes on the problem and the stakes are raised. It is either

an "UP" moment that turns downward at the end, or a "DOWN" that turns upward at the end.
ROSE DIES SUDDENLY AND EILIS IS RIDDEN WITH GUILT FOR NOT BEING THERE.

10. Bad Guys Close In <u>Section</u> (pgs. 55-75): There may be no specific "bad guys," but the PROBLEMS should get worse and worse – the main character seems to be <u>failing</u> in their approach, and/or is facing more and more seemingly impossible obstacles. Things escalate with their antagonistic forces, often with a "punch-counterpunch" feel (their relationships with allies tend to break down, too). Note the page count here — this section, along with Set-up & Debate, Fun & Games, Finale, are made up of multiple scenes, and represent big chunks of the movie.
SHE GETS A CALL FROM HER MISERABLE MOTHER TELLING HER SHE MUST COME BECAUSE MOTHER CANNOT BE ALONE. TONY IS AFRAID SHE WON'T COME BACK TO HIM AND SHOWS HER LAND HIS FAMILY PLANS TO DEVELOP FOR THEIR HOMES.

11. All Is Lost (pg. 65). The story seems to be over, and the main character seems to have no hope now. The main problem of the story seems to have been answered in the negative. Everything they were trying has failed, and they have <u>no other options</u>. Things are worse than ever before.
CONFUSED, EILIS SAYS SHE MUST GO HOME BUT DOESN'T KNOW WHERE HOME IS ANYMORE.

12. Dark Night Of The Soul. (a moment in All Is Lost)
FEELING GUILTY, SHE WONDERS WHY SHE LEFT IRELAND. TONY IS AFRAID SHE WON'T COME BACK; SHE

TELLS HIM SHE DOESN'T THINK SHE HAS A HOME ANY-
MORE.

**13. Break into Act Three (pg 85). A new idea, a new hope,
a new plan for solving the story problem emerges (often
the A Story and B Story "cross" – the B Story should also
be <u>unresolved and at its worst</u>).**
SHE AGREES TO MARRY TONY BEFORE SHE GOES TO IRE-
LAND. AT COURTHOUSE THEY MEET A MAN WHOSE
WIFE HAS FAMILY IN EILIS' HOME TOWN. THEY ARE
A SECRETLY MARRIED COUPLE WITH NO PLACE TO GO.

**14. Finale <u>Section</u> (pgs. 85-110): A five-part challenge akin
to "storming the castle to rescue the princess." The hero
fails at first, and is pressed to their absolute limit – forced
to confront their own demons, and possibly change their
approach to life – before the story problem is finally
resolved.**
EILIS BACK IN IRELAND. SHE MOURNS ROSE, CAN'T
SHARE WITH ANYONE THAT SHE IS MARRIED. HER
MOTHER IS EXPECTING HER TO STAY, EVEN ACCEPTS AN
INVITATION TO EILIS' BEST FRIEND'S WEDDING. HER
SISTER'S FIRM OFFERS HER AN ACCOUNTING JOB. EILIS
MEETS JIM. HE'S YOUNG, WEALTHY AND AVAILABLE.
SHE ENJOYS SEEING HIM, EVERYONE HINTING HE'S
A GOOD CATCH. SHE DOESN'T ANSWER TONY'S
LETTERS BECAUSE SHE DOESN'T KNOW WHAT TO SAY.
SHE'S TORN WISHING IT HAD BEEN THIS WAY BEFORE
SHE LEFT.

HER NASTY OLD BOSS, MRS.KELLY, FINDS OUT ABOUT
TONY AND THINKS SHE CAN USE THIS KNOWLEDGE TO
BLACKMAIL EILIS. EILIS REALIZES THIS PETTINESS IS

WHY SHE LEFT IN THE FIRST PLACE AND BOOKS A
SHIP HOME. SHE TELLS HER MOTHER THE TRUTH AND
LEAVES.
ON BOARD SHIP, SHE HELPS ANOTHER IRISH GIRL
MANAGE THE VOYAGE AND ENTRY INTO AMERICA.

**15. Final Image. Reflecting the new status quo now that
this story is over.**
SHE'S AT HOME WITH A FUTURE IN TONY'S ARMS.

*"A census taker once tried to test me.
I ate his liver with some fava beans
and a nice chianti."*

—Hannibal Lecter, *Silence Of The Lambs* (1991)

Step Three.

Find your **subplots** through your characters.

We've covered the beginning, Acts I, II and III, plot points and the midpoint. Which brings us to a saleable screenplay's next essential ingredient: Subplots.

After I tell you what I've learned about subplots you will never take them for granted again.

A subplot is just what it sounds like: A short plotline which plays a *secondary or "B" role*, but is related to the main plotline by expanding its theme. Even if a subplot does not intersect directly with the "A" story, it must reflect it in some way. Here are some characteristics of subplots:

1. A subplot must have at least three narrative beats, one in each of the three acts, but can have many more beats.

2. A subplot must have a beginning, middle, and end.
3. Subplots typically have a specific point or points of intersection with the main story, but it is not essential as long as they have a connection to the theme of the main story.
4. Subplots can provide multiple points-of-view.

No one in a script, not even Tom Hanks in *Castaway*, lives in a total vacuum. He had the character "Wilson", a basketball he talked to, and the picture in his stopwatch of his girlfriend, the beautiful Helen Hunt. We all have people around us and situations that make us who we are, make us do what we do. Good movie characters have the same elements.

Subplots, created from our supporting characters, bring us to fear and tears and laughter. They make us FEEL. I cannot emphasize this too strongly. Subplots make us FEEL. Subplots raise the emotional stakes and make your movie sing.

Once you get this, the construction of your scripts will come more easily, and make more sense to you. Your "A" story of course is your protagonist's main thrust. After that, all subplots are called "B" stories. In order of importance you can have the "A" story, a "B" story, a "C" story and so on. But be wary. Too many subplots complicate a film. They make a film harder to follow and thus sell unless you're George Clooney, who sold a whopper of a complicated plot in *Syriana*.

Every good movie has memorable subplots. Say you're writing a movie about Ann, a young woman of 25 who's been in therapy since her teens because of an uncle who molested her as a child. What does she want in the story? She wants to get her master's degree in psychology. She wants to help people like she was helped. That's your "A" story. Okay. Now what?

Now we add the subplots by creating the supporting characters and the antagonist, the person who threatens to take what she wants away from her. Let's say, she rents her brother's car to get to school but it's always broken down. She refuses to pay for a vehicle that doesn't work and demands he get it fixed. They fight. She blames him for never looking out for her, even as a kid. He saw what her uncle did to her but never helped. He claims he was too scared himself to do anything. This is a subplot.

At school, one of Ann's teachers starts hitting on her. She needs to be nice, she thinks, to get a good grade, but her professor is pushing for a date and because of her background she begins to feel very uncomfortable. This is a subplot.

A fellow student goes off the deep end and holds Ann and the professor as hostages. This is a subplot.

Feeling guilty, her brother comes to school to talk to her and discovers the fellow student holding them at gunpoint. He knows the fellow student and it's revealed they have had a relationship that stemmed from this same uncle molesting the brother as well. Ann is shocked but finally understanding of her brother's fears as a child. He tries to save his sister this time and in the scuffle gets seriously wounded. She and he mend their anger and both heal from the experience.

All of the subplots resonate from the theme of the story which has to do with power struggles stemming from Ann's experience as a child.

Where do subplots always come from? They come from our supporting characters. The characters that we create to tell our story.

There's a huge, very important difference between the "A" story and the subplots or "B" stories.

The "A" story thread is what gives the film its direction and thrust. It is the motor or the engine of the story. The "B" stories give us complication, depth and emotion. The "B" stories move our characters and I'll say it again. They move us to FEEL and therefore get us involved.

Michael Landon, The Father I Knew, is a television movie I wrote and co-produced for American television that ended up being released as a feature in Europe. It is the story of Michael Jr. trying to regain the place in his father's heart he occupied before Michael Landon Sr. chose a new woman and had a second family. After Michael Sr. is diagnosed with much publicized fatal liver cancer, Mike Jr. needs to find a cure, tell his father he still loves him, and hopefully, hear these same words from Dad before he dies.

There were six Landon children and I only had time to reveal the most meaningful stories out of the six. After interviewing Lynn Landon, Michael Jr.'s mother, and his sister, Leslie, we focused on their relationships with Michael Sr. and with each other. It is a heart-wrenching story of children's emotional survival after being abandoned by a parent, especially a famous one.

In order to work, subplots must mirror, reflect or impact the main story in some way. Each scene must move the story forward. Let me give you some examples:

The Fighter took four years and four writers (Scott Silver, Paul Tamasy, Eric Johnson and Keith Dorrington) to bring its characters to life. After his older brother, Dickie Eklund, is imprisoned for drug abuse, Irish Mickey Ward returns to the ring to step out of his brother's shadow and win the success for his family that his brother sabotaged when he was fighting. The "A" story through-line is Mickey wants to fight and win. But check out the subplots that touch our every emotion.

1. Enter his manager mother who wants to control his every breath and who we love to hate.
2. Beware his five bouffanted, bawdy and brawling sisters

who become a Greek chorus to his journey, and will beat up anyone they perceive to be in his or their way.

3. Behold his up and down relationship with his screwed up but idolized brother, Dickie.

4. Observe his growing relationship with the woman he loves who hates his family and who is hated by them in return.

Every subplot reflects the fighter in all of them and echoes what he's fighting for.

In *Up In The Air,* George Clooney's Ryan Bingham is a guy who has no attachments whatsoever. His goal is to accumulate as many sky miles as he can to acquire a membership in a special airline club. It is a straight forward through-line. Now, adding subplots based on the supporting characters brings us to a place where we look inside ourselves. A good subplot will get us to say "I've done that." "I've felt that way." Let's look at the subplots:

1. Ryan Bingham's world is shaken when his boss tells him he has to come off the road and introduces a woman whose plan is to keep him in the office permanently. This is a disaster. How will he ever reach his goal if he doesn't travel?

2. Along the way, he keeps getting emails from his sisters, whom he hasn't seen in years, regarding a wedding which he doesn't believe in, and doesn't want to attend.

3. Squeezed in between, Ryan meets a woman who's his exact unemotional, unattached match. He falls hopelessly in love with her, only to find out that she's married.

There are subplots galore that all reflect the fragility of relationships and Ryan's fear of them. These subplots that bring heart, pain and laughter are necessary to a very unemotional "A" story.

In *American Beauty*, the "A" story is: Lester Birnham wants to get his body into shape so his daughter's girlfriend will go to bed with him. Remember? That was it, straight forward, no emotion in it. He digs out his old gym equipment and starts working out in the garage. Let's look at the subplots.

1. Carolyn, his shrewish wife, played brilliantly by Annette Benning, ropes us in emotionally when she viciously tears into him for being a disappointment while she battles self-esteem issues of her own.
2. Jane, his daughter, seemingly hates him, but really wants him to love her.
3. Jane pretends that Ricky Fitts, the camera geek next door, bugs her but is secretly attracted to him.
4. Ricky, who is beaten senseless by his Marine father, Colonel Fitts, pretends he is a waiter but sells dope.
5. The macho Colonel turns out to be a closet gay and his wife has gone so deep inside in denial, she is practically catatonic.

Subplot heaven. All reflecting Lester's low self-esteem and his deciding to do something about it.

We are torn by emotions that come not from the "A" story but the "B" stories. The "A" story on its own would be quite dry, but supported by the "B" and "C" subplots, the movie becomes rich in emotion.

Do you see now how every subplot reflects or impacts or counterpoints the theme of winning and losing of the "A" story?

Subplots are also guided by the three act paradigm's directional markers. You intersect the stories as needed to build the film as a whole to the most dramatic conclusion.

Each subplot also has to have a beginning, middle, and end. They don't have to have the detail necessary in the "A" story, but enough to satisfy the audience so that the thread doesn't just disappear. You've seen those bad movies, or badly edited movies, where you find yourself asking," Hey what happened to the guy that …?" or "What happened to the sister that stole the key that opened the safe that…"

Be careful not to get so carried away by your subplots that the focus veers from the "A" story. The subplots should support the "A" story, not detract from it. If you get too deep into a subplot, you may have to check your story again. If a supporting character becomes more important than your protagonist, maybe you're telling the wrong story.

You'll find out once your characters tell you. And they will.

"I am big. It's the pictures
that got small."

—Norma Desmond, *Sunset Boulevard* (1950)

Step Four.

Create interesting characters.
Heroes, Bad Guys, Point Of View

Characters are what keep our butts in the seats at the movies or glued to the tube at home. Can you think of a beloved character from a movie that comes to mind? Try to think of the characters and not the actors that played them.

To mention just a few, who can forget Birdman, Forrest Gump, Peter Pan, James Bond, Atticus Finch, Hannibal Lecter, Jack Sparrow or Edward Scissorhands? How about Michael Corleone or Han Solo? And there's Rhett Butler and Ratso Rizzo and Superman. And on the ladies' side we have *The Hunger Games'* Katniss Everdeen, Vivian Ward, the ultimate *Pretty Woman*, Miranda Priestly, the she-devil who wore *Prada*, Tinkerbell, Thelma and Louise, The Wicked Witch of the West,

Nurse Ratched, Baby Jane, Bridget Jones, Norma Rae, Juno and Scarlet O'Hara. Why are these characters so unforgettable?

Unforgettable characters are relatable. There's a part of you in them and they cause us to think and feel. We care about them, but most importantly: we believe them.

Think in terms of the real people you know, or people you have observed, and what makes them unique. Part of the intrigue are their habits and mannerisms. Maybe they are foul-mouthed, but funny. Maybe they wear their shoes too large and slop around in them as they walk. Perhaps they have a permanent kind smile or a sparkling attitude. Maybe they keep their dentures in their shirt pocket and not their mouths, or like my old boss, Barry Diller, they play constantly with a rubber band on their fingers.

What if your character quotes movie dialogue or giggles when they talk? What if they have an amazing vocabulary, can tell great stories, but they bitch about everything? What if they kill without hesitation or remorse? What if they see dead people?

You want your audiences to watch your characters and say, "I've been there." or "I want to be there." or "I wonder what 'there' is like?" The closer you stay to yourself or people you know or have observed, the more believable your characters will be.

If you believe, like directors Walter Hill and Clint Eastwood, that a character is what he does and not what he says, then you'll start building that character from their actions. Then try to figure out how they became that way or what experiences shaped them.

Take *Gran Torino* for example. Eastwood's character, the lonely disgruntled Korean War vet, Walt Kowalski, sets out to reform his neighbor, Thao, a young Hmong teenager, who tried to steal Kowalski's prized 1972 Gran Torino. At the beginning of the film, he's a trigger-happy, racist old fart. At the end, he's the same guy but his racism has shifted from hating his quiet, Hmong neighbors to protecting them from the gang bangers that have taken over his neighborhood.

The Hmong's are grateful, and an affection grows between them and Walt, but he stays the same unforgiving, bitter, aged badass he is at the beginning of the film. Rather than the Hmongs changing him, he changes them by turning Thao into a man. Soon it's clear that Walt loves Thao and his family, but he goes right on calling them "chinks". It's not out of spite or anger, just the way it's always been with Walt. It's what he does.

Gregg McBride, an MTV teen comedy writer, creating stories using fourteen to seventeen year olds, always has got to find a way to distinguish between them. In a contribution to Final Draft's *Ask The Pros*, he recounts this delightful story:

"I recently had to create a big sister character whose main function in the script was to drive her little sister around. I wondered how I could make the big sister more interesting in such small snippets of time? That's when I came up with making her a devotee of Christian Rock – but with self-burned CDs that replace the name of Jesus with the name of her boyfriend. Just a cute little quirk but one that made the character memorable."

Memorable indeed, Gregg. As screenplay writers, we learn to look at what the characters do — to see if they work. I don't mean what they do with their hands in a given scene, I mean what they do to move the story along. Do they give us information we didn't have before? If they aren't the protagonist, our good guy on his or her mission, and they're not the antagonist, the bad guy, whose job it is to stop the mission, what do they do? Do they support or hinder as they change the course of the story? You must certainly write literal activity for the actor in your scenes, but that can likely be changed by the director and the actor themselves on the set. What they do is what they do to make the story move forward.

Without active characters whose actions move the story along, you have little or no chance to create a workable film. When choosing your characters, ask yourself, "How do they move the story forward?" If they don't move it, lose them. If too many of your characters are doing the same thing, hit the delete button or combine them all into what is called a **COMPOSITE CHARACTER**.

Whenever I see the words composite character I think of this story: I wrote and produced a series pilot, *Rio Shannon* starring Blair Brown (*Fringe*), Michael Deluise (*Encino Man*) and Penny Fuller (*All The President's Men*) for ABC. It was based on a box of dusty papers a hotelier named John Egan had stuffed under his bed. It was the book he'd never shown anyone about his life as a blue-eyed boy from Cincinnati who fought reverse discrimination in a sea of New Mexican brown. John Sacret Young (*China Beach*) was my executive producer and Mimi Leder (*Deep Impact, Pay It Forward*) directed.

Before I sat down to write, I researched the town, talked to all of the family members, read and re-read John's manuscript and then wrote a two-hour movie based on him and his family's adventure. After reading my first draft, a studio exec told me there were too many characters and I had to combine the two sisters into one. This is a real live family and I had grown close to them all. I felt like an assassin when I deleted the character "Morgan Cleary" from my computer. To make her feelings known, the real Egan sister wore a tee shirt on the set every day that screamed, "BRING BACK MORGAN CLEARY!"

In a good screenplay, the writer's job is to keep the characters busy and involved. Too many characters and you'll be spinning your wheels trying to find something for them all to do.

Characters are the light in the eyes of your screenplay. You should know them like a second skin before putting pen to paper. Know everything about them, even their past lives if applicable.

Let's look at your main characters.

There's obviously the protagonist, the main man or woman we are rooting for — YOU if it's a life story or memoir.

The antagonist(s) who represent(s) the conflict. We need lots of conflict or we have no action and without action, we have no story.

And there's the third type of character: the **CATALYST OR SUPPORTING CHARACTERS** who carry out an action or give information to move the story forward. You all know catalyst characters —the best friend, the bartender, the judge, the taxi driver, the manicurist, the boss, the assistant, the teacher, the Queen Mum. Yes, the Queen Mum. Not the Queen, but her mother who appeared just when the Queen needed sage advice to move the story forward.

Since the plot must center on the lead character and follow his or her journey, all catalyst characters should either support the protagonist or the antagonist or move the plot. If they do not serve any of these functions, find your delete key.

Both the protagonist and the antagonist need to change in the course of your story through conflict and the story's resolution. In order to make them change, you have to know them, really know them. The supporting characters should change as well and have depth no matter how few lines they get. **Remember, they never follow storylines of their own that do not involve the main character.**

If you really trust in the process, your characters will form themselves, but here's how to help them along.

It's imperative to write character bios (3-10 pages) for each of your characters. A lot of beginning screenwriters think they don't need to do this, then they wonder why they can't think of anything to write in the middle of Act II. They come up short because they don't really know their people.

Out of your bios – your characters' pasts – comes history, core attitudes, point of view, personality, habits and a sense of purpose.

Don't make the mistake of assuming the bad guys don't need as much character detail — they do, particularly in motivation. Sure a story about a killer is suspenseful and scary, but if you have a killer who kills because he was locked in a closet for the first five years of his life, it makes the story that much richer. Even the bad guys have motivations that seem good to them. Didn't Charlie Sheen really think he was saving the world from trolls? Your antagonist should too.

To get answers that surprise you about your characters, do what I do. Interview them. Don't let your friends see you do this or they'll call the guys with the straight jackets. Take some time to sit down at the keyboard, or with your notepad, and interview your characters. Ask the questions out loud and then write down the answers you hear in your head. Ask everything even though you think you know the answer.

Where were they born, what schools did they go to? How many siblings? What recognitions have they earned? What are they ashamed of? Are they good-natured or sad sacks? What would they change about themselves? Why haven't they? What is their avocation? What is their vocation? Will they ever do what they really want to do?

Listen to the answers then read between the lines. How are they different in their personal, professional and private lives? What are they most afraid of? What will they fight to protect or fight to avoid? How are they at a party? What would they do watching TV alone? Animals? Habits? Quirks? What do they want? What runs them? If you don't know what they want, how can you create obstacles to them getting it? What is their point of view? Is their glass half full or half empty? Are there patterns to their behavior? Do they do the same thing over and over and wonder why nothing changes? How can these traits work for you in the dramatic telling of your story?

Is your character brave like Jamal Malik in *Slumdog Millionaire* who risks his life to get the girl? Or is he a coward like Carter Burke who'd do anything to protect his company's bottom line in *Aliens*? What's your character's POV (point of view)? Does he or she think they can only succeed by breaking rules or following them? What are their values, their belief systems?

Our POV is the way we look at the world. It's what separates one person from another. If your character is a parent, then he or she may have a parental POV. Do your characters have the point of view of a student, a rich kid or a terrorist?

To get the reader and the audience to care about your character, you must put the audience inside the character's point of view with him so that they feel like what's happening to that character is happening to them. For it to become an emotional journey, the audience needs to experience what your characters think, feel and want from inside the character's POV. It's not enough for them to be mildly interested. They have to really care about and relate to this human being and really want him to achieve his or her goal. Don't write so the audience observes the story, write so that the reader experiences and feels what's going on in the story.

To determine your characters' POVs, ask them questions about the story and their lives. Why do they need to do what they are doing? What will happen if they don't succeed?

Why do you need to do this? Because it helps you iron out the wrinkles in your character's motivation and your story's construction. If you interview your character and he reveals a motivation that seems weak to you, great.

Now you have a chance to fix it before you've slaved over 100 screenplay pages.

Ask yourself what happened to make these people who they are when they arrive on page one in your screenplay. Syd Field calls this their "interior life." An interior life is what you have created by writing the characters biography. It is a process that <u>forms</u> character.

We teach that the "exterior life" of your character takes place from page one of your screenplay until the conclusion. It is a process that <u>reveals</u> character.

What happens to who they are from page one to the end is called the character's arc. Characters in a good story have a set of outside obstacles to deal with and also a set of internal obstacles to deal with. How well you play one against the other is how deeply invested your audience will be.

The "rule" that there must be conflict in every scene often leads newer writers astray into thinking every scene must be an argument. This is not the case. Some of the most powerful conflicts are internal. It is your job to present that struggle.

Many catalyst or supporting characters are used to move the story along, but don't make them stick figures. Give all characters the same meticulous attention. Who can forget the poor gas station owner played by Gene Jones out in the boonies who had to face the vicious Anton Chiguhr played by Javier Bardem in *No Country for Old Men*? Jones only had one scene but I thought about him long after the movie ended. And he did absolutely nothing but react in total horror as he comes to the conclusion he could be dead in a blink of an eye.

And there is, of course, Dame Judi Dench in *Shakespeare in Love*. She won an Academy Award for only one eight minute scene, but she was drawn so carefully by the writer that it knocked us out. And what about Julia Child's adoring, supportive husband in *Julie and Julia* played by Stanley Tucci or

Hannibal Lecter's smarmy nemesis, Dr. Frederick Chilton played by Tony Heald in *The Silence of the Lambs?* He was the guy who would end up providing the protein in Hannibal Lecter's fava beans and a little Chianti. It was a small role but it provided what little comic relief the film held.

It remains controversial as to its meaning, but what about the last scene in *Birdman* where Michael Keaton's daughter looks up out of his hospital window and smiles? Did he fly away? Had he died the day before? Did he climb up the side of the building? Whatever your take, it is a hard scene to forget.

And if you saw *The Revenant*, I am sure the bear scene will stick to your cerebral lining for some time. And even the steaming bear skin scene, might give you pause.

The scene in *Spotlight* that remains in my gray matter is the one where Rachel McAdams' character has tracked down an ex-priest who was charged with molestation. When she asks him about his crimes, he tells he didn't get anything out of it. As if his lack of sexual pleasure gave him the right to recuse himself.

Supporting characters should be as memorable and written with as much care as the leads in your film. They aren't just props, but help the main characters do their jobs.

Remember, characters are defined by what they do, not by what they say. A lover can say, "I love you, I love you, I love you," but it's when he pulls the trigger and blows off her head that we discover who he really is.

What characters *do* to get their needs met makes them who they are. What obstacles you put in their way and how they deal with them makes them who they are. Good characters are people we care about, and most importantly *people we believe*. An audience will first identify with the character before the story. You must write characters that an audience can connect with. And that takes dialogue. But dialogue is not the movie. The story is the movie.

When you're deep in the process of writing your script, it should take from twenty to thirty pages for the characters to start talking to you. Yep. They start telling you what they want to do, what they want to say. Once they've made contact, they'll take over. Let them do what they want to do. You are still in charge because you know where the delete button is.

Sometimes, characters even want to alter your story line. Let them do it. The worst that can happen is that you'll realize it didn't work. But it's important to take the detour, because out of accidents and detours sometimes comes magic. You may discover something you never even thought of. Something sensational.

After turning in my first draft of *Almost Golden: The Jessica Savitch Story*, I was given a note by my executive producer, Bernie Sofronski, (*Another World, Murder in Mississippi*) to make Jessica more likeable. Likeable? I had researched her for months, read every book written about her, looked at old footage and talked to anyone who knew her that was still alive and willing to talk. She was a drug addled bitch on wheels with father issues and then she died. How was I to make her more likeable? Much to my amazement, my first attempt at making her likeable worked. I simply gave her a sense of humor. Her ability to laugh at herself and make others laugh took the edge off her driven character just enough for us to like her.

"You had me at Hello."

—Dorothy Boyd, *Jerry Maguire* 1996

Step Five.

Find your theme and style. What ties it all together?

What is theme in screenplay? The theme is the principle or lesson that underlines the overall story. Theme is the message you want to tell the reader, the foundation of your entire script. Every good film is about something. And that something is a theme that winds its way through the material, an idea that deepens the storyline and characters. It's the writer's job to constantly *prove* the theme.

Themes are sometimes called a life lesson or a message, and the best ones are always subtle. You don't want to preach or harangue your audience with THEME in Capital Letters. You want your readers (the buyers), then your audience (film-goers) to realize it in their own time, which is usually after the movie ends.

Some producers, directors, and writers approach the idea of theme immediately while others let their theme emerge as the story progresses. *Time Magazine* says, "Steven Spielberg's parents divorced when he was 19 years old, an incident that clearly affected the young man. In his films, *Close Encounters of the Third Kind, Indiana Jones and the Kingdom of the Crystal Skull,* fatherhood is something to be feared, avoided and run away from...until it isn't. An older Spielberg has said that, had he been a father at the time, he would have thought twice about having the main character in *Close Encounters* abandon his family so quickly".

The marketing people behind *Witness* claim their theme is, "Love cannot bridge the gap between two different worlds." In *The African Queen*, the opposite is true. "*Love **can** bridge the gap of two different worlds.*" Here are some other movie themes:

Aladdin
Deep down, people are more than what they seem, and Aladdin must accept who he is.

Avatar
Jake says, "All I wanted in my sorry-ass life was a single thing worth fighting for."

Room
Innocence lost. How far will a mother go to protect her son's innocence?

Up in the Air
Many of the fired people talk about their families. Ryan has no family. He says, "To know me is to fly with me. This is where I live." Ryan has no home. Travel is his home. And the audience asks, "Let's see if that is going to change!"

It's good to know your theme before you start the screenplay because the entire story hinges on it. It is the result of the decision the protagonist ultimately makes at the end of the picture and it is the **opposite** of what he or she wants. Confused?

In *Little Miss Sunshine,* the father believes that winning is good, losing is the enemy. He wants nothing but success for his family and won't accept anything else. Look to the end of the picture to see that the theme is just the **opposite**. At the end of the story, Olive fails in her attempt to win the pageant, but the family grows stronger and closer as a result of it. Loving is more important than winning and exactly the theme of the movie and the lesson the father needs to learn.

In *127 Hours*, Aron Ralston, the isolationist hiker, wants to get away from everyone and sets out into the wilderness for a rejuvenating weekend. At the end of the film, he's learned the biggest lesson of his life. The theme becomes the opposite of what he wanted, and he realizes no man is an island. It becomes a film about hope and rebirth and happily being a part of something, in this case – a family.

In *The King's Speech,* King George VI (Bertie), plagued by a dreadful stammer and insecurities from childhood, wants to remain an obscure royal rather than take on a hugely public role as King after his brother abdicates. Through a set of unexpected techniques learned from a commoner he comes to admire as an equal, Bertie conquers his issues and leads the country through war. The resulting theme being: It takes leadership to confront a nation's fear and friendship to conquer your own.

In *Juno*, determination really paid off even though she got one and not the two parents she had hoped for. The theme for Juno has been said to be: growing up means making tough decisions. Remember to put your character on a path that will land him or her at exactly the point the theme is trying to make by the end of the story.

To help you understand the concept, read this good example from the script consultant/managers at Michael Feris' Script-A-Wish (Scriptawish.com http://scriptawish.com);

> "*When Rick puts Ilsa on the plane and walks into the sunrise with Reneau, the theme of Casablanca might be said to be, "We can have both a rich inner life and a rich outer life, if we choose love over romance." In other words, when we choose real love. That's why Rick says, "We'll always have Paris." He's not choosing the greater good over love; he's choosing both his love for Ilsa and the ability to serve the world. He's evolved into something opposite the freedom fighter he was in Spain and the head-over-heels boy he was in Paris at the beginning of the film. He's a new, far more responsible man.*"

There's nothing wrong with finding the big picture theme first, then honing it to fit your particular story.

To help keep you on track, write the theme at the top of every page or tack it above your desk to remind you where you're going and to include the theme wherever possible as you construct your action and write your dialogue. Being constantly aware of your theme will also keep you from writing yourself into a corner, or sending mixed messages to your audience.

What is **STYLE?** Your style of writing is your voice. It is the way you see and hear your script playing out and how that translates to each page of your script.

Style cannot be taught, but it can be copied. The best way to help you see the difference in style is to look at Jim Brooks and Mel Brooks. They both write and direct comedy but the style in which they write their comedy is totally different. Compare Mel's *Blazing Saddles* with Jim's *As Good as It Gets* and you'll see what I mean.

Mel Brooks uses broad campy slapstick while Jim Brooks uses intimacy and fear-of-intimacy in his interactions to make us laugh. Their style is the way they personally feel about humor and how they see their comedy playing out on screen.

You need to set up your style in the first three pages or three minutes as I mentioned earlier. When formatted properly, each page of your screenplay is considered one minute of screen time.

If you're writing a black comedy, where topics and events are regarded as forbidden, (specifically those related to death) and are treated in a humorous or satirical manner while retaining their seriousness, you've got to take the audience by the hand and spell it out right away: "Hey, this-in-your-face insensitive-rudeness is supposed to be funny and make you uncomfortable!" The same for thrillers, mysteries, romances.

Once you set up your style, stick with it. No changing it up in the middle or near the end. Remain committed. There's nothing that spells out amateur faster than a screenwriter changing their style from quirky comedic scenes to dark, murderous and deadly (or vice versa) in the middle of the piece. Style is sometimes confused with class or with genre. A genre is a type of film, a class or category. Style is the way you write that particular genre in your own personal voice.

"Will you look at that! Look how she moves! It's like Jell-O on springs..."

—Jerry, *Some Like It Hot* (1959)

Step Six.

Write effective dialogue!

In Hollywood's golden years, Billy Wilder really made his mark with *Some Like It Hot*, *The Seven Year Itch*, *Double Indemnity* and *Sunset Boulevard*. He was a master of dialogue in both drama and comedy.

Today, I think Aaron Sorkin is the greatest dialogue master of his generation. If you want to hear his music for yourself, rent *A Few Good Men*, *Malice*, *The American President* or *Charlie Wilson's War*. Listen to this aria from Colombia Pictures' *The Social Network* based on the book, *The Accidental Billionaires* by Ben Mezrich. In this scene, Mark Zuckerberg (Jesse Isenberg) is being deposed by the lawyer, Gage.

> GAGE
> Let me re-phrase this. You sent my clients 16
> e-mails. In the first 15, you didn't raise any concerns.

                        MARK
Is that a question?

                        GAGE
In the 16th e-mail you raised concerns about the
site's functionality. Were you leading them on for
six weeks?

                        MARK
              (beat)
No.

                        GAGE
Why hadn't you raised any of these concerns
before?

                        MARK
              (quietly)
It's raining.

                        GAGE
I'm sorry?

                        MARK
It just started raining.

                        GAGE
Mr. Zuckerberg, do I have your full attention?

                        MARK
No.

> GAGE

Do you think I deserve it?

> MARK

> (beat)

What.

> GAGE

Do you think I deserve your full attention?

> MARK

I had to swear an oath before we began this deposition and I don't want to perjure myself so I have a legal obligation to say no.

> GAGE

Okay. "No" you don't think I deserve your attention.

> MARK

I think if your clients want to sit on my shoulders and call themselves tall they have a right to give it a try. But there's no requirement that I enjoy sitting here listening to people lie. You have part of my attention—you have the minimum amount. The rest of my attention is back at the offices of Facebook where my colleagues and I are doing things that no one in this room, including and especially your clients, are intellectually or creatively capable of doing. Did I adequately answer your condescending question?

I heard Aaron Sorkin say in an interview that his parents started taking him to Broadway shows at the age of nine. Though he didn't fully understand the messages in *That Championship Season* or *Who's Afraid of Virginia Wolfe?* he understood he loved the rhythm of the words.

Good dialogue does have rhythm and pace and each character's rhythm should be different, so that when you read a script, you hear a full orchestra of melody and counterpoint. The main purpose of dialogue is to move the story forward! Remember, film is a visual medium and characters are what they DO more than what they SAY. So why does everyone make such a fuss about the words our characters speak? Because those words have many other jobs as well.

Dialogue also:

1. reveals character.
2. reveals conflict and tension between and within your characters.
3. establishes relationships.
4. provides commentary about the action.
5. reveals emotional states. Dialogue helps make us laugh, cry, shudder, squirm. It makes us FEEL.

Quentin Tarantino is another master of cutting to the quick with his dialogue. I heard it said once that if you took the macho stance of *Reservoir Dogs*, the very cool, Travoltaness of *Pulp Fiction*, throw in the revenge of *Kill Bill*, set the film in World War II – you'd get Universal Pictures' amazing *Inglourious Basterds* (sic). Listen to the rhythm of this speech Brad Pitt delivers as Lt. Aldo Raine:

LT. ALDO RAINE

My name is Lt. Aldo Raine and I'm putting together a special team, and I need me eight soldiers. Eight Jewish-American soldiers. Now, y'all might've heard rumors about the armada happening soon. Well, we'll be leaving a little earlier. We're gonna be dropped into France, dressed as civilians. And once we're in enemy territory, as a bushwhackin' guerrilla army, we're gonna be doin' one thing and one thing only...killin' Nazis. Now, I don't know about y'all, but I sure as hell didn't come down from the goddamn Smoky Mountains, cross five thousand miles of water, fight my way through half of Sicily and jump out of a fuckin' air-o-plane to teach the Nazis lessons in humanity. Nazi ain't got no humanity. They're the foot soldiers of a Jew-hatin', mass murderin' maniac and they need to be dee-stroyed.

Even though Tarantino gives Raine a backwoods cadence, his intention is crystal clear. You know for sure "...them Nazis they're gonna die".

Dialogue is a feature of character. If you know your characters well enough, they will speak to you by themselves. And yet, writing good dialogue is an acquired art. You might write clunky, on-the-nose dialogue at first. New screenwriters often tell what they are supposed to show. But don't despair, the more you do it, the easier and better it gets.

You have to get to the meat of each scene and show it moving the story forward. Obviously small talk can be used as a character's avoidance of an issue, but make sure it isn't just disjointed babble.

Learning to write good dialogue requires a lot of listening. Sit quietly in a public place and pay attention to what people are saying. Don't listen just to words, listen to phrasing, to rhythm and to pitch. Very few people speak in clear, concise sentences. Record people talking then transcribe it word for word. You'll hear that most of our sentences aren't even finished before the other person responds, nor do we speak in complete sentences or always use verbs. My friend, a fine writer and writer's consultant, Dorothy Randall Gray (*Soul Between The Lines: Free Your Creative Spirit*) says, "Only twenty percent of communication consists of the words spoken. The rest is delivered in body language". After you transcribe your recording, you'll realize that without body language and inflection, most real dialogue reads like gibberish.

Listen to these exchanges between Vivian and Edward in Buena Vista Pictures *Pretty Woman* written by J. F. Lawton and Stephen Metcalfe. Many responses are incomplete sentences:

INT. HOTEL - ELEVATOR - NIGHT

The young ELEVATOR OPERATOR is dressed in a clean red uniform that seems just a bit too tight. As the elevator doors close he nods toward Edward.

OPERATOR

Evening, sir.

EDWARD

Good evening. Penthouse.

VIVIAN

Penthouse. My, my.

She sees the operator glancing at her.

                    VIVIAN

The penthouse. And step on it.

After Vivian tells Edward how badly she was treated while
shopping, he takes her to a fashion boutique. Listen to this
subtly hilarious exchange. Can't you just hear a drummer
delivering rim shots?

                    EDWARD
You see this young lady over here?

                    HOLLISTER
Yes.

                    EDWARD
 Do you have anything in this shop as beautiful as
she is?

                    HOLLISTER
Oh, yes.
        (Edward gives Hollister a look.)

                    HOLLISTER
Oh, no! No, no! No. I'm saying we have many
things. As beautiful as she... would want them
to be!
        [babbling]
That's the point I was getting at. And I think we can
all agree with that. That's why, when you came in
here, you knew from the first—

EDWARD

You know what we're gonna need here? We're
going to need a few more people helping us out.
I'll tell you why. We are going to be spending an
obscene amount of money in here. So we're going
to need a lot more help sucking up to us, 'cause
that's what we really like.

HOLLISTER

Ohhhh!

EDWARD

You understand that?

HOLLISTER

Sir, if I may say so, you're in the right store, and the
right city, for that matter! Exactly how obscene an
amount of money were you talking about? Just…
profane, or really offensive?

EDWARD

Really offensive.

HOLLISTER
(to himself)
I like him so much.

EDWARD

I think we need some major sucking up.

HOLLISTER

Very well, sir. You're… not only handsome, but a
powerful man. I could see the second you walked
in here, you were someone to reckon with…?

                        EDWARD
        Hollister

                        HOLLISTER
        Yes, sir?

                        EDWARD?
        Not me. Her.

Do you hear that short staccato sentences are mixed with longer passages to give us this script's particular rhythm? Try reading a script a week. Ideally, you'll read twenty! Listen to the rhythm the writer uses. Rhythm is part of each writer's style.

Here's a list I have put together over the years for when I am asked to talk about good dialogue. Let your characters:

1. interrupt, lie and exaggerate.
2. talk over each other or overlap, as we call it in the trade.
3. avoid answering directly. Let your characters be distracted. Just like in real life, have a character pretend they don't hear at first to buy some time.
4. use the wrong words occasionally (malapropos).
5. misunderstand.
6. do not try and write an accent.

I know Tarantino did it in the example I just showed you from *Inglourious Basterds*, but he IS Quentin Tarantino and you're not. When and if you get as many paying jobs as he has, you can write with an accent. Better to simply identify in parenthesis under the character's name (thick southern drawl) or if it's appropriate for the character, (rich Irish brogue). You can write <u>dialogue</u> that's indigenous to the areas but not the <u>dialect</u>. Let the actor do that.

7. and finally, only use perfect grammar if the character demands perfect grammer. No one, in real, every day life, speaks with perfect grammar unless they're giving a speech on perfect grammar! Not even the man who would be King.

For example, listen to these scenes from The Weinstein Company's *The King's Speech* written by David Seidler. Seidler writes the first stammer and then advises the audience (for ease of reading) that he will no longer write the stammer. Colin Firth who played Bertie, was directed to stammer by Tom Hooper. In an interview from a behind the scenes special, *The Making of The King's Speech,* Colin Firth says that Hooper made him stammer on every line. It was a terrific challenge and he could not do it. Some lines came out clean and clear no matter how he tried to mess them up. As a result, the creative team feels now, it came across as a very real impairment.

CARD: (*this means words are printed on the screen for the audience to read*)

1925 King George V reigns over a quarter of the world's population. He asks his second son, the Duke of York, to give the closing speech at the Empire Exhibition in Wembley, London.

INT. BBC BROADCASTING HOUSE, STUDIO - DAY

CLOSE ON a BBC microphone of the 1920's, A formidable piece of machinery suspended on springs.

A BBC NEWS READER, in a tuxedo with carnation boutonniere, is gargling while a TECHNICIAN holds a porcelain bowl and a towel at the ready. The man in the tuxedo expectorates discreetly into the bowl, wipes his mouth fastidiously, and signals to ANOTHER TECHNICIAN who produces an atomizer. The Reader opens his mouth, squeezes the rubber bulb, and sprays his inner throat. Now, he's ready. The reader speaks in flawless pear-shaped tones. There's no higher creature in the vocal world.

> BBC NEWS READER
> Good afternoon. This is the BBC National Programme and Empire Services taking you to Wembley Stadium for the Closing Ceremony of the Second and Final Season of the Empire Exhibition.

INT. CORRIDOR, WEMBLEY STADIUM – DAY

CLOSE ON a man's hand clutching a woman's hand. Woman's mouth whispers into man's ear.

> BBC NEWS READER (V.O.)
> 58 British Colonies and Dominions have taken part, making this the largest Exhibition staged anywhere in the world. Complete with the new stadium, the Exhibition was built in Wembley, Middlesex at a cost of over 12 million pounds. The Exhibition has attracted over 27 million visitors from every corner of our great Empire and the rest of the world.

INT. CONTROL ROOM, BBC BROADCASTING HOUSE - DAY

Technicians in suits, ties and scientific looking overcoats, wearing bulky headphones, monitor daunting banks of valves and dials while the Reader continues:

>   BBC NEWS READER (V.O.)
> Today the vast Stadium is filled to capacity with in excess of 100,000 spectators...as regiments from His Majesty's Army, Navy and Air Force stand in review.

INT. GREEN ROOM - DAY

Nervous eyes flick towards a tunnel leading to a bright light.

CLOSE ON - BERTIE - the Duke of York, second son of the King; his handsome, sensitive, features look terrified.

>   BBC NEWS READER (V.O.)
> The Opening Ceremony was the first occasion his Majesty the King addressed his subjects on the wireless. The close of the first Season was the initial time His Royal Highness the Prince of Wales had broadcast. And today His Royal Highness the Duke of York will give his inaugural broadcast to the Nation and the World.

WIDEN TO REVEAL his young wife, truly an English rose.

>   ELIZABETH
> Time to go.

He stares straight ahead, frozen. She gives him a loving peck on the cheek, quickly rubbing off a fleck of lipstick.

                    BBC NEWS READER (V.O.)
          Leading us in prayer will be the Right Honourable
          and Most Reverend Archbishop of York, Primate of
          all England and Metropolitan. Now we go live to
          Wembley Stadium, where His Royal Highness the
          Duke of York will read his message from the King.

COSMO LANG - comes up to Bertie. Tries to be helpful but makes him more nervous.

                    COSMO LANG
          I am sure you will be splendid. Just take your time.

The last bars of "God Save The King" echo down the corridor.

ROBERT WOOD, the Chief BBC Engineer on location whispers:

                    WOOD
          Let the microphone do the work, sir.

Wood checks his watch.

                    WOOD (CONT'D)
          Thirty seconds, sir.

Bertie braces his shoulders manfully, but without an ounce of confidence, closes his eyes, nods, opens them, and reluctantly goes through the tunnel towards the light,

like a prize-fighter entering the arena, to be greeted by
the roar of the crowd.

EXT. ROYAL PODIUM - DAY

HAND-HELD CAMERA, BERTIE'S POV: far ahead, at
a seemingly impossible distance, is the huge intimidating
microphone, the only thing between the terrified
observer and 100,000 people.

Silence falls over the stadium.

Overhead, thick roiling clouds.

BERTIE approaches...like a death march.

Bertie's eyes widen in terror as he reaches the microphone. The red transmission light blinks four times then
glows solid red. Bertie is live.

INT. CONTROL ROOM, BBC BROADCASTING
HOUSE – DAY

Technicians stare at dials and listen to the hiss of silence.
The Reader and Floor Manager glance at each other
nervously.

EXT. SPECTATOR STAND, EMPIRE STADIUM -DAY

In the tense silence PAN THROUGH some of the crowd
waiting with growing discomfort. In particular we notice
a father and son watching intently.

EXT. ROYAL PODIUM - DAY

Bertie is frozen at the microphone. His neck and jaw muscles contract and quiver.

> BERTIE
> I have received from his Majesty the K-K-K

(For ease of reading, Bertie's stammer will not be indicated from this point in the script)

The stammer careens back at him, amplified and distorted by the stadium PA system. (CU below means close up)

CU huge metal speakers.

CU soldiers at rigid attention.

CU Wood, he shuts his eyes.

CU Cosmo Lang, expressionless.

CU Elizabeth, dying.

Bertie gulps for air like a beached fish and attempts to continue:

> BERTIE (CONT'D)
> ...the King, the following gracious message...

He can't get the word out. SPLAT...the first drops of rain begin to fall.

Notice how David Seidler writes so efficiently about the emotion generated by Bertie's problem. He simply notes Elizabeth is "dying." But we all know how embarrassed she is for the man she loves. Note this next scene that takes place in Westminster Abby where the King (Colin Firth) and Lionel Logue (Geoffrey Rush) are rehearsing for his coronation.

Lionel sits down on the chair of Edward the Confessor.

> BERTIE (CONT'D)
> What're you doing? Get up! You can't sit there!

Overlapping—(*this means the writer wants the actors to talk over each other.*)

> LIONEL
> Why not? It's a chair.

> BERTIE
> No, it's not, that is Saint Edward's Chair-

> LIONEL
> People have carved their initials into it!

> BERTIE
> That chair is the seat on which every King and Queen-
> LIONEL
> It's held in place by a large rock!

> BERTIE
> That is the Stone of Scone, you are trivialising everything-

> LIONEL

I don't care. I don't care how many Royal arses have sat in this chair-

Overlapping—

> BERTIE

Listen to me... !

> LIONEL

Listen to you?! By what right?

> BERTIE

Divine right, if you must! I'm your King!!!

> LIONEL

Noooo you're not! Told me so yourself. Said you didn't want it. So why should I waste my time listening to you?

> BERTIE

Because I have a right to be heard!

> LIONEL

Heard as what?!

> BERTIE

A man! I HAVE A VOICE!!!

> LIONEL
> (quietly)

Yes you do. You have such perseverance, Bertie,

you're the bravest man I know. And you'll make a
bloody good King.

Notice how the character of Lionel Logue is revealed by
how he prods the king's internal struggles. We learn that
he's caring enough to risk his friendship with the king to
build a deeper one. By discovering that when the king gets
really angry, he speaks more clearly, Logue is helping to build
his confidence. We learn so much about both men by this
simple exchange.

8. all your characters should speak a little differently. See if
   you can assign distinctive speaking patterns to single
   characters. If you're a stand up comic, don't make them
   all wise crackers. Let just one character have the jokes.
9. make your dialogue realistic by having most characters'
   speech informal and contain occasional profanity. We
   use "guy" instead of man, "bucks" instead of dollars and
   lots of contractions and dropped letters; e.g. "goin",
   y'know." Here's an example from Polygram's masterpiece, *The Big Lebowski* written by the wittily profane
   Ethan Coen. Notice how the inquisitor is kept out of the
   shot so his disembodied voice seems more threatening.

INT. BEDROOM - NIGHT

The Dude enters and flicks on a light. His head is
grabbed from behind and tucked into an armpit.
We track with him as he is rushed through the living
room, his arm holding the satchel flailing away from
his body. Going into the bedroom the outflung satchel
catches a piece of doorframe and wallboard and rips
through it, leaving a hole.

The Dude is propelled across the bedroom and on into
a small bathroom, the satchel once again taking away
a piece of doorframe. His head is plunged into the toilet.
The paper bag hugged to his chest explodes milk as
it hits the toilet rim and the satchel pulverizes tile
as it crashes to the floor.

The Dude blows bubbles.

> VOICE
> We want that money, Lebowski. Bunny said you
> were good for it.

Hands haul the Dude out of the toilet. The Dude blubbers
and gasps for air.

> VOICE
> Where's the money, Lebowski!

His head is plunged back into the toilet.

> VOICE
> Where's the money, Lebowski!

The hands haul him out again, dripping and
gasping.

> VOICE
> WHERE'S THE FUCKING MONEY, SHITHEAD!

> DUDE
> It's uh, it's down there somewhere. Lemme take
> another look.

His head is plunged back in.

> VOICE
> Don't fuck with us. If your wife owes money to
> Jackie Treehorn, that means you owe money to
> Jackie Treehorn.

The inquisitor hauls the Dude's head out one last time
and flops him over so that he sits on the floor, back
against the toilet.

The Dude gropes back in the toilet with one hand.

Looming over him is a strapping blond man.

Beyond in the living room a young Chinese man unzips
his fly and walks over to a rug.

> CHINESE MAN
> Ever thus to deadbeats, Lebowski.

He starts peeing on the rug.

The Dude's hand comes out of the toilet bowl with his
sunglasses.

> DUDE
> Oh, man. Don't do—

> BLOND MAN
> You see what happens? You see what happens,
> Lebowski?

The Dude puts on his dripping sunglasses.

DUDE

Look, nobody calls me Lebowski. You got the
wrong guy. I'm the Dude, man.

BLOND MAN

Your name is Lebowski. Your wife is Bunny.

DUDE

Bunny? Look, moron.

He holds up his hands.

DUDE

You see a wedding ring? Does this place look like I'm
fucking married? *All my plants are dead!*

I'm not suggesting you need to drop the F-bomb every
other line, but occasionally, profanity can define a character.

10. bust all of your clichés unless it works for one character.

What cliché clichés am I talking about? You know them:
about face, bent out of shape, all ears, airing dirty laundry,
anything goes, dressed to the nines, all that jazz, all that glit-
ters, good as gold, as the crow flies, back in the day, a penny
saved is a penny earned, make a smile your umbrella, all in a
good day's work, children should be seen, not heard. Do I look
like I am made of money? Were you raised in a barn? Idle
hands are the devil's workshop, etc. Bust them, please.

Do not use exposition in your dialogue. For example, if you have a scene where a bank robbery is taking place, don't have someone say: "Oh look, that guy is robbing us!"

Instead go to your action paragraph and describe what is going on. Perhaps you describe how your character's mouth drops open and he is too frightened to even speak. Then cut to the bank robbers at the door with their Uzis pointed directly at the character's heart. It's much more effective to SEE it rather than to HEAR about it.

 Look at how much we learn about Clarice Starling's character as well as Hannibal Lecter in this exchange from Ned Tally's screenplay for Orion Pictures', *The Silence of the Lambs*. Remember their deal? He'll trade information about the killer she's looking for if she gives him personal information about herself. In this scene she is standing far outside his cell.

> DR. LECTER
> No. It's your turn to tell me, Clarice. You don't have any vacations to sell on Anthrax Island. Why did you run away from that ranch?

> CLARICE
> Dr. Lecter, when there's time I'll -

> DR. LECTER
> We don't reckon time the same way, Clarice. This is all the time you'll ever have.

> CLARICE
> Later, listen, I'll -

> DR. LECTER
> I'll listen now. After your father's murder, you were

orphaned. You were ten years old. You went to live
with cousins, on a sheep and horse ranch in
Montana. And - ?

> CLARICE
>
> And - one morning I just - ran away...

She turns from him. He presses closer, gripping the bars.

> DR. LECTER
>
> Not "just," Clarice. What set you off? You started
> what time?

> CLARICE
>
> Early. Still dark.

> DR. LECTER
>
> Then something woke you. What? Did you
> dream...? What was it?

IN FLASHBACK

The 10-year old Clarice sits up abruptly in her bed,
frightened. She is in a Montana ranch house; it's almost
dawn. Strange, fearful shadows on her ceiling and
walls...a window partly fogged by the cold; eerie
brightness outside.

> CLARICE (V.O.)
>
> I heard a strange sound...

> DR. LECTER (V.O.)
>
> What was it?

THE CHILD RISES

crosses to the window in her nightgown, rubs the glass.

> CLARICE (V.O.)
> I didn't know. I went to look...

HIGH ANGLES (2ND STORY) - THE CHILD'S POV

Shadowy men, ranch hands, are moving in and out of
a nearby barn, carrying mysterious bundles. The men's
breath is steaming. A refrigerated truck idles nearby,
its engine adding more steam. A strange, almost
surrealistic scene...

> CLARICE (V.O.)
> Screaming! Some kind of - screaming. Like a child's
> voice...

THE LITTLE GIRL

is terrified; she covers her ears.

> DR. LECTER (V.O.)
> What did you do?

> CLARICE (V.O.)
> Got dressed without turning on the light. I went
> downstairs... outside...

THE LITTLE GIRL

in her winter coat, slips noiselessly towards the open barn door. She ducks into the shadows to avoid a ranch hand, passes her with a squirming bundle of some kind. He goes into the barn, and she edges after him reluctantly.

> CLARICE (V.O.)
> I crept up to the barn... I was scared to look inside – but I had to...

THE LITTLE GIRL'S POV

as the open doorway LOOMS CLOSER... Bright lights inside, straw bales, the edges of stalls, then moving figures...

> DR. LECTER (V.O.)
> And what did you see, Clarice?

A SQUIRMING LAMB

is held down on a table by two ranch hands.

> CLARICE (V.O.)
> Lambs. The lambs were screaming...

A third cowboy stretches out the lamb's neck, raises a bloody knife. Just as he's about to slice its throat -

BACK TO THE ADULT CLARICE

staring into the distance, shaken, still trembling from the child's shock. We see Dr. Lecter, over her shoulder, studying her intently.

                    DR. LECTER
They were slaughtering the spring lambs?

                    CLARICE
Yes...! They were screaming.

                    DR. LECTER
So you ran away...

                    CLARICE
No. First I tried to free them... I opened the gate of
their pen - but they wouldn't run. They just stood
there, confused. They wouldn't run...

                    DR. LECTER
But you could. You did.

                    CLARICE
I took one lamb. And I ran away, as fast as I
could...

IN FLASHBACK

 a vast Montana plain, and crossing this, a tiny figure -
the little Clarice, holding a lamb in her arms.

                 DR. LECTER (V.O.)
Where were you going?

                 CLARICE (V.O.)
I don't know. I had no food or water. It was very
cold. I thought - if I can even save just one... but he
got so heavy. So heavy...

The tiny figure stops, and after a few moments sinks to the ground, hunched over in despair.

> CLARICE (V.O.)
> I didn't get more than a few miles before the sheriff's car found me. The rancher was so angry he sent me to live at the Lutheran orphanage in Bozeman. I never saw the ranch again...

> DR. LECTER (V.O.)
> But what became of your lamb?
>   (no response)
> Clarice...?

BACK TO SCENE

as the adult Clarice turns, staring into his feverish eyes. She shakes her head, unwilling - or unable - to say more.

> DR. LECTER
> You still wake up sometimes, don't you? Wake up in the dark, with the lambs screaming?

> CLARICE
> Yes...

> DR. LECTER
> Do you think if you saved Catherine, you could make them stop...? Do you think, if Catherine lives, you won't wake up in the dark, ever again, to the screaming of the lambs? Do you...?

CLARICE
Yes! I don't know...! I don't know.

DR. LECTER
(a pause; then, oddly at peace)
Thank you, Clarice.

There is no other place in the structure of this film that we could possibly learn all of this personal information about Clarice nor her vulnerability. It also shows the brilliant perception of Lecter's character and how his facile yet sick mind can destroy his victim's defenses.

11. make sure you use dialogue that is true to the period in which you are writing

Take a look at these various exchanges from Joel and Ethan Coen's screenplay adaptation of Charles Portis' 1968 novel for Paramount Pictures, *True Grit.* Note the formality and unfamiliar, vintage vernacular, true to the period.

MATTIE ROSS
You must pay for everything in this world, one way and another. There is nothing free except the grace of God.

ROOSTER
We'll sleep here and follow in the morning.

MATTIE
But we promised to bury the poor soul inside!

ROOSTER

Ground's too hard. Them men wanted a decent
burial, they should have got themselves killed in
summer.

LUCKY NED PEPPER

What is your intention Rooster? You think one on
four is a dogfall?

ROOSTER

I mean to kill you in one minute, Ned. Or see you
hanged in Fort Smith at Judge Parker's conven-
ience. Which will you have?

LUCKY NED PEPPER

I call that bold talk for a one-eyed fat man!

ROOSTER

Fill your hand you son-of-a-bitch!

Did you notice that true to period, much of the language is
direct and to the point without frills or embellishments?

Let's look at a movie where there are no other characters to
speak of besides the leading man. How does he relate information without having someone to talk to? He uses a video
camera! Listen to these monologues spoken by Aron Ralston's
character in *127 Hours* written by Danny Boyle and Simon
Beaufoy (based on the book *Between a Rock and a Hard Place* by
Aron Ralston), for Fox Searchlight Pictures.

ARON

Hey there, Aron! Is it true that you didn't tell
anyone where you were going

ARON

Good morning, everyone! It's 6:45 Tuesday morning in BJ Canyon! The weather is great. I figure by
now that Leona, my housemate - Hi, Leona!- has
missed me hopefully since I didn't show up last
night. Another hour and a half they'll miss me for
not showing up at work... Hi, Brion at work! Best
case scenario is they notify the police and after
a 24 hour hold they file a report, a missing person's
report. Which means noon tomorrow it's official
that I'm gone. I do still have the tiniest bit of water
left. Well, actually, I've resorted... I've had a couple
pretty good gulps of urine that I saved in my
Camelbak. I sort of let it distill... It tastes like hell.
So, it's 70 hours since I left on my bike from
Horseshoe Trailhead during which time I have
consumed 3 liters of water, a couple of mouthfuls
of piss...

ARON

Mom, Dad, I really love you guys. I wanted to take
this time to say the times we've spent together have
been awesome. I haven't appreciated you in my
own the way I know I could. Mom, I love you.
I wish I'd returned all of your calls, ever. I really
have lived this last year. I wish I had learned some
lessons more astutely, more rapidly, than I did.
I love you. I'll always be with you.

In this way, director Danny Boyle (*Slumdog Millionaire*) and
actor James Franco provide us with the interior struggle as well
as the exterior struggle of a man trapped by a huge bolder in
no man's land.

Writers always think their dialogue is so fresh and clever. I remember working with Jane Seymour on a film I co-wrote and co-produced for Universal called *Matters of the Heart*. She taught me a lesson. It was a May-December love story with Jane as the beautiful older woman to Christopher Gartin's handsome young man. We were sitting in Jane's trailer on location in Montecito, California, and I was helping her run her lines (memorize them). She was a consummate professional and rarely, if ever, did not know her lines word for word. But one particular line kept sticking in her throat. She had trouble saying it. Not because it was difficult. The line was something like, "Love is never easy." When we talked about why, Jane didn't mince words. She told me straight out.

"In my career, do you know how many times I've had to say that same line? All writers think they are so clever, but you all say the same thing!"

Needless to say, I busted what I learned was a cliché from the mistress of romance movies. Which brings me to an unspoken rule: Say things differently if you can, from character to character. And try to always say more with less words. Make every word of dialogue count and use them to reveal, instruct, entertain and inform your audience.

"Find a truly original idea. It is the only way I will ever distinguish myself. It is the only way I will ever matter."

—John Nash, *A Beautiful Mind* (2001

Step Seven.

Build good scenes using the proper form.

T here's only one way to write a scene that Hollywood executives recognize as standard in format and content. If you have been reading scripts as I have suggested, you will see that for every line there is a purpose. Structure is everything in screenwriting and so is form. I suggest buying a screenwriting program to take care of form for you and I recommend FINAL DRAFT or MOVIE OUTLINE.

What is a scene? A scene is a unit of action in your screenplay. Its purpose is to move your story forward by delivering at least one new element of information to your audience. It can be major information: the patient dies of a heart attack; or it can be as simple as the chiming of a clock to show the passing of time.

Why are scenes so important? Because they move your story with action and reveal character, and because good scenes are unforgettable. Very often, rather than the entire story, we only remember scenes from the films we love. How about the scene in which Aron Ralston cuts off his own hand in *127 Hours?* Remember the "Run Forrest Run!" scene in *Forrest Gump?* It's hard to forget the meltdown scene in *Frost/ Nixon* where Richard Nixon finally admits his failure to the world, or the look on Carey Mulligan's face when she realizes her fiancé is already married in *An Education*.

The key ingredient here is *new*. Unless you're writing *Groundhog Day* where almost every scene was repeated verbatim to make a point, every scene should reveal some new aspect of our characters or provide new information to move the story.

Scenes can be as short or as long as you want them. The story/plot (these terms are synonymous) determines their content and length. If you get lost, ask yourself, "What needs to happen in this scene to move my story? What is its purpose?"

There are two types of scenes: Action scenes where something happens visually, or dialogue scenes. Most scenes combine the two, action and dialogue. You can have one without the other.

Every scene has a beginning, middle and end and a conflict and a resolution, but you don't have to show all of it. You can enter mid-fight, or in the middle of a sex scene or murder if you want. You get to choose.

Remember. Your first scene or scene sequence in the picture is extremely important. A scene is a segment of film that usually takes place in a single time and place, often with the same characters. Scene and sequence can usually be used interchangeably, though the latter term can also refer to a longer segment of film that does not obey the spatial and temporal unities of a single scene.

For example, a montage sequence shows in a few shots a process that occurs over a period of time. It has to be a grabber in action, content, style and tone, because it sets the pace of the entire script.

Good examples of two scene sequences that don't open the film are the wedding sequence in *The Godfather* and the drug bust sequence in *Goodfellas*. They are all the same "scene" but shown from different angles in different locations.

There are three elements in all scenes:
1. **Location**: Where does your scene take place?
2. **Time of day**: In film, you have only two choices: day or night.
3. **Are you inside or out**? In film, there is only INT. for interior, or EXT. for exterior. If you change either place or time, it is a new scene.

When you change time or place, it becomes a new scene designated by what Final Draft calls a slug line. Slug lines contain INT. or EXT. (inside or out), the location, and whether it is day or night.

Not Dead Yet is a romantic comedy I wrote about a reality show producer who is hiding the recent death of his fiancée from all of his coworkers except one. The fiancée returns in three-dimensional succulent flesh to lead him to the woman he should marry.

This is the opening sequence that introduces the reality show mansion, NOAH, our producer and lead, his new assistant, GRACIE, his cameraman, ALMIGHTEE, and HARRY, a carpenter, who are all in the basement of the mansion when we meet them. We INTERCUT the scenes of them with the scenes of the emcee of the show, LIAM, inside the foyer and the scenes of the DIRECTOR in the video truck parked outside

the house. You always capitalize NAMES the first time you
introduce characters. I'll point out some other sign posts and
terminology as I go along.

FADE IN: (*This literally means the first image of the movie
comes into sight*)

ESTABLISHING – DAY (*This is a slug line. "Establishing"
means an overall shot of the location.*)

A mega "reality show" (*a popular type of 21st century television show*) mansion with pool, tennis courts, imposing
driveway filled with video trucks and equipment. Its giant
double doors are open and various crew members move
in and out. (*this is the exposition of the scene that tells us
what we are looking at*)

INT. VIDEO TRUCK (*a video truck is a van-like vehicle used
on location to house the recording equipment and the director
who watches the recorded action taken inside the house on
remote TV screens in the truck*)–SAME–(*means at the same
time as the slug line in front of it*) INTERCUT (*means we will
cut back and forth between this and the location listed in the
slug line above it*)

INT. VIDEO TRUCK – SAME – DAY – INTERCUT

The DIRECTOR (30's) on a headset and crew sit at
monitors showing the foyer staircase. (*Always capitalize
the name of a character the first time we see them and
note their age.*)

> DIRECTOR (*character's name*)
> Rehearsal from the top, people. Liam's intro.
> Screens down...

INT. FOYER – SAME – INTERCUT

A bank of big screen TVs descend from the ceiling above and behind a grand staircase. All flash the logo, "HE/SHE."

VIDEO TRUCK

> DIRECTOR
> Liam in position.

On the monitor, LIAM CLOONEY (30's), an Irish heart-throb with blonde tips, hits a mark at the top of the staircase.

> LIAM
> Hello, hello, you lucky people.

> DIRECTOR
> And...lights up!

INT. MANSION BASEMENT – SAME – INTERCUT

Blackness. We hear urgent TAPPING and MUFFLED VOICES as if from behind a wall.

> NOAH (O.S.) (*this means the voice is heard Off Screen*)
> Light! Where's the light?

> GRACIE (O.S.)
> We're buried alive down here!

> NOAH
> We're losing time. God, Almightee, where are you?!

VIDEO TRUCK (*When you intercut in a sequence it is under-stood that you are still in the same place as was previously established. You do not need to keep typing INT or DAY as long as you remain in the same sequence.*)

The director, oblivious to the drama in the basement, carries on with his rehearsal.

> DIRECTOR
> Okay Liam, think excitement, think mystery, think provocative.

STAIRCASE

> LIAM
> (loving it)
> Think dirteeeeeee.

INT. BASEMENT

The scene is now illuminated by what seems like a searchlight cutting through thick fog. The fog shudders, then explodes. Dirt and plaster fly. Shrouded shapes appear and disappear in the moving dust. As the light finds them, we can make out three dim figures.

NOAH DUNCAN (34), a TV producer wrapped a little too tight, peers through a gaping hole in a wall bashed in by HARRY (40) a beefy carpenter. Noah's got that boy/man look that women like more than they know why.

                    NOAH
          (to the man holding the light)
     Almightee, bring that work light closer! Hurry up!

ALMIGHTEE GARZA (24) a man of few words, and a body that would make Madonna weep, pulls his light into position.

                    ALMIGHTEE
     Dude.

He gets a little too close to GRACIE MINTZ (25) in surgical mask, sunglasses and scarf.

                    GRACIE
     Hey, watch the shoes! You know how much these cost?

VIDEO TRUCK

The director, still oblivious to the drama in the basement, continues his rehearsal.

                    DIRECTOR
     And that's... ACTION.

STAIRCASE

Liam's voice deepens as if announcing something important.

                    LIAM
        Ten hopefuls compete for a quarter of a million
        dollar jackpot. And will they have to work for it!
        Welcome to America's most provocative new show
        where a bold few will do the unthinkable...where
        a bold few will destroy...

BASEMENT

Harry whacks another wall with a sledge hammer. As the
dust clears, Noah steps through the opening.

                    NOAH
        What's this? More dressing rooms?

Gracie and Harry follow. Almightee works his light.

ALMIGHTEE'S POV (*This means what he sees from his point
of view.*)

An underground living area, circa 1920's. We see books,
boas, theatre posters, a satin gown, even flapper panties
laid out on the bed. It's home sweet home except for the
dust and cobwebs.

                    GRACIE
        It's more like an apartment. A lady's apartment.
        Look, lingerie, jewelry...

She opens an ornate jewelry box. We hear a strange WHOOSHING sound. Almightee ducks and makes the sign of the cross.

ALMIGHTEE

Dude!

Gracie begins to cough. Everyone reacts to a smell.

GRACIE

That smell! What is it? Roses?

Almightee pulls his shirt off to cover his nose.

NOAH

Old roses! Awful! Close it!

GRACIE

Fine. You don't need to yell.

She slams the box closed and moves deeper into the apartment.

STAIRCASE

The bank of HE/SHE logo screens morph from the show's logo into pre-taped action VIDEOS of ten men: lifting weights, fighting a fire, arm wrestling, sawing wood, driving a bull dozer, etc. (*this means the images on the TV screens change from a printed name of the show's logo into live action footage of men doing various activities.*)

> LIAM
Ten of the country's manliest men will strive to
prove they're man enough to be UNMANLY as well!

BASEMENT

Noah daintily lifts a tea bag from a tea cup on a table set
for two. Harry pulls out plans from his back pocket.

> HARRY
This space wasn't here when the house was
designed in '27. Looks like it was carved out later.

> NOAH
So why would you go to all that trouble, then wall
it off with two feet of cement?

Gracie screams. Almightee faints. Noah grabs the light
and aims it at the bedroom area. A skeleton lays on
top of the bed.

> NOAH (CONT'D)
To hide a body. Of course.

And off Gracie's face in total shock.

STAIRCASE

Images of the He/She men continue to flash behind Liam.

> LIAM
Who will be brave enough to reveal his most secret
fears and obsessions? The same fears that your

husbands and boyfriends out there are hiding!
Watch out, America, this is HE/SHE!

BASEMENT — LATER

We TRACK Noah and Gracie upstairs. (*Track means we
follow them with a camera*) They ignore POLICE taping
over the basement stairs, a PARAMEDIC treating
Almightee, a DETECTIVE grilling Harry. Reality show
chaos: glitzy gowns, wigs pushed by on racks, make up
stations, cables, lights, etc.

> NOAH
> I need two shows in production in a month, I don't
> have time for a dead flapper. Is there a show in
> dead flappers?

> CONTINUOUS:
> (*Continuous means the action doesn't stop and camera
> keeps following.*)

As they walk, Gracie sheds her mask, scarf and shades,
revealing brunette perfection on four-inch Manolos.
(Manolo Blahnik is the name of a very expensive shoe.)

> GRACIE
> Chill, handsome. You've got He/She in great
> shape and Last Psychic Standing auditions
> tomorrow at four.

> NOAH
> Paranormal's been done to death. It's a failed idea,
> like Two and a Half Men without Charlie Sheen.

> GRACIE
>
> I believe in the paranormal and Daddy loves ghost shows. Daddy thinks it'll be a hit. And if Daddy thinks it'll be a hit, you need to make it a hit.

> NOAH
>
> Gracie, screw your daddy.

> GRACIE
>
> (barely a whisper)
>
> I'd rather you screw me.

> NOAH
>
> Not going to happen.

> GRACIE
>
> (smiling)
>
> That's what you say.

> NOAH
>
> Ever.

Because all of the scenes on this opening sequence intercut back and forth in the same sequence and time frame, it is not necessary to write INT. or EXT. for each time we intercut. Nor is it necessary to put in CUT TO: after each scene. Going to a new slug line denotes a new scene because it is a new location.

Before you begin each scene, remind yourself of the context which means the conditions under which the scene takes place. In other words, what goes on between the scenes that you don't write. Now, since I know my characters as well as the back of my hand, I know what happened to Noah and

Gracie before they came to work and my knowing that informs the scene. At this point, only I know why Noah is such a grump. Sure, he's under pressure to get two reality shows off the ground, but there is something else that colors his reaction to the comely Gracie that only I know.

It makes sense, doesn't it? I mean if you don't know what goes on with your characters between scenes, who does?!

Another example – did your character pay a visit to her shrink off screen and then on screen decide to break up with her boyfriend because of what the shrink said? She may never mention it in that scene but it will come up and be revealed at some point. Did your lead win the lottery and not tell anyone as she picks up the lunch check and buys all of her girlfriends new cars? Did your male lead get promoted and have a martini to celebrate before he meets with his son's teacher? Is that why he is inappropriately intimate? Did your protagonist stop to try on bathing suits, none of which fit, and by the time she gets to her dinner date can't eat a thing? Only you know the context for the scene.

After you know the context, and you have decided on purpose, place and time, the content of the scene will follow. Content means the combination of action and dialogue that moves our story forward. Be mindful of how the scene starts and ends. Are we hooked enough to read the next scene or have you given away the plot? Listen to what your characters say to you! And if you know them well enough and have done your research, they will tell you what to write next.

Here is an excerpt from *Michael Landon, The Father I Knew,* a script that I wrote for CBS Television. Lynn Landon has just watched her estranged husband, Michael Landon, receive an Emmy. After the awards she follows him to the home of his mistress then returns home. As you read, see if you can determine the purpose of each scene.

INT. BEVERLY HILLS HOUSE, FOYER — LATER

Lynn, emotionally drained, enters. Leslie runs down the stairs.

>   LESLIE
> Mom, wasn't it great that dad won!?

Lynn fights them, but the tears come anyway.

>   LESLIE (cont'd)
> What is it? What happened?

Outside we hear the FERRARI. (*you must capitalize any SOUND that the sound department needs to note so that they can make a proper recording of it.*) Lynn quickly retreats out of sight. Confused and upset, Leslie swings open the front door. Michael Sr. enters, also looking distraught.

>   LESLIE (cont'd)
> What's with Mom? What's going on?!

Dad motions for Leslie to sit down on the stairs next to him.

>   MICHAEL SR.
> Les, you know how much I love you. It hurts me to even say it, but

>   LESLIE
> Dad, what's happened?!

                        MICHAEL SR.
            I've lived like a priest in this business.

                          LESLIE
            What are you talking about?

                        MICHAEL SR.
            I've met a woman and fallen in love with her.

Leslie processes this impossible bit of news.

                    MICHAEL SR. (cont'd)
            Don't hate me. Please.

A gut-wrenching animal noise explodes from Leslie and
she begins to sob. His own tears stream down Dad's face.

                          LESLIE
            No. God, no.

                        MICHAEL SR.
            Please, please don't hate me. I couldn't handle that.

Lynn, astonishingly composed, reappears in the foyer.

                           LYNN
            What are you telling her? — Leslie, go to your
            room.

Still sobbing, Leslie runs up the stairs. Michael Sr. moves
to Lynn, She distances him with her arms. He's racked
with confusion, guilt.

CONVERSATIONS OVERLAP

> LYNN (cont'd)
> What did you say to her?!

> MICHAEL SR.
> I want her to know the truth!

> LYNN
> The truth? What is the truth, Mike? That you just led me to the apartment of the woman you're sleeping with.

> MICHAEL SR.
> I didn't lead you anywhere. You followed me!

> LYNN
> You said the affair was over!

> MICHAEL SR.
> And you knew it wasn't. I invited you to be with me tonight. My offer didn't interest you.

> LYNN
> Because you've been giving me such mixed messages! Why am I not enough for you, Mike?! After all these years, I don't understand?!

> MICHAEL SR.
> You don't have to understand. Just accept it.

> LYNN
> Accept that you've chosen someone else over...

MICHAEL SR.
(anguished, he interrupts)
It's not you! It's me. I'm not excited anymore by
what I do. None of it gives me any pleasure and it's
tearing me apart. I know people see me differently,
but I feel like — a nothing.

LYNN
And me, what do I feel? What do I do?

MICHAEL SR.
You look the other way.

LYNN
How can you be so selfish? We've built
something here!

MICHAEL SR.
And I've given you everything you asked for and
lived like a saint, damn it!

LYNN
A lifestyle, a family, a place in our community...

His hands go to her throat as if he can choke her into
understanding.

MICHAEL SR.
And now I want her, Lynn. Her innocence, her
excitement about my work, her...

> LYNN
> Her youth – will not bring back yours! No matter
> how you stage it, or cast the players, you're going
> to have to let go of that poor, abused little boy
> inside of you. Why can't you let him grow up and
> old with me?

Michael Sr. steps away. Lynn holds her own throat now as
if to hold in what's left of her from seeping out. She can
barely whisper.

> LYNN (cont'd)
> I don't deserve this.

> MICHAEL SR.
> But I do. I deserve you both.

Silence. The sound of real truth seeking it's own level.
Finally:

> LYNN
> Get out. Just get out.

He exits. Lynn sinks to the floor, racked by sobs. Their
lives altered forever.

INT. BEVERLY HILLS HOUSE, MIKE JR.'S ROOM –
SAME

Jr.'s sound asleep, oblivious to his family being torn apart
and spared the SOUND of LESLIE CRYING next door.

EXT. BEVERLY HILLS HOUSE, DRIVEWAY –
NEXT DAY

Leslie, behind the wheel in her new '80 white Mustang,
brings Mike Jr. from school. He's out before her. She drags
herself to the door.

                    MIKE JR.
          What's wrong with you today?

                    LESLIE
                 (dazed, numb)
          Nothing.

                    MIKE JR.
          Nothing? You haven't said a word all day. You're
          acting like somebody died.

She pushes past him and rings the doorbell. Both she and
Mike are shocked to see Uncle Bob open the door.

                    MIKE JR. (cont'd)
          Uncle Bob, what are you doing here?

His eyes red from crying, his face somber, Bob hesitates
enough to indicate something is very wrong.

                    UNCLE BOB
          Come inside. We need to talk.

INT. BEVERLY HILLS HOUSE, LIVING ROOM –SAME

They all take a seat as Bob struggles for the words.

UNCLE BOB
Your Dad's gone. He and your mom are having
serious problems. She's upstairs hurting really
badly. She needs you.

Mike Jr. so stunned, he can't even move. He looks to
Leslie but she's too damaged to speak. All there is to do –
is to go to Mom.

INT. BEVERLY HILLS HOUSE, MASTER BEDROOM –
SAME

The kids move through the door. Lynn, raw, looking like
all life has been sucked out of her, stands in the middle of
the room. She opens her arms to them. Their closeness
triggers Leslie and Lynn to sob, but numb, in shock,
Mike Jr. feels nothing.

INT. MICHAEL LANDON'S MALIBU HOUSE, DEN –
DAY

The room, full with family, is as we left it. Adult Mike
Jr.(ACTOR # 3), watches Cindy holding his father's thin
shoulders. Jr. reflects:

MIKE JR. (V.O.)
I wonder, Dad, if you knew how painful it was
going to be, if you would have still left us.
So painful for Leslie that she blocked it altogether.
So painful to Mom, she rarely left her room...

INT. BEVERLY HILLS HOUSE, OUTSIDE MASTER – DAY

The kids play on the landing. Their father hammers on Lynn's door.

MICHAEL SR.
Lynn, I'm not leaving until you let me in!

A "click" and he pushes through the door, closing it behind him.

MIKE JR. (V.O.)
...so surreal and indefinable to me that my role model was drifting farther and farther away. It was like a slow death and we were all watching.

This movie was directed by Michael Landon Jr. who faced the world's wrath as he bravely told the story of what it was to be "Little Joe's" real-life son and how it hurt to be replaced by Michael Landon's new family. As sad as the story was, it was an honor for me to get to know the family and be able to work on this project.

During the days I spent writing Michael Landon's death scene, I checked in with his family and the doctors multiple times to make sure I got it right. Out of respect and caring for Michael's ex-wife, Lynn and son, Michael Jr., I worked hard to get not only the emotion right — the delicate balance of fear and pain and sadness that permeated not only the whole house, but the masses of fans who gathered outside standing vigil and those around the world. And, just as important, I wanted the technical jargon to be accurate. Before I started writing, I thoroughly researched Michael's disease, a liver cancer called adenocarcinoma, until the medical lingo became more and more familiar. At the time, it was only lingo to me. Now I cringe as I write the word.

How could I know that upon completion of that research, and that scene, I too would be diagnosed with cancer? One that had no cure. Was it some sick cosmic coincidence? Had I literally created the illness by focusing so hard on the subject? Had I taken my own good health and good fortune for granted?

I had finished the first draft of the script. CBS had signed off and we were about to go into production when I got word that I had CML, chronic mylogenous leukemia. I needed to start treatment immediately. Besides being the writer, I was the co-producer on the project. My duties didn't end when I wrote Fade Out. Rather, a whole new set of puzzles were to be solved by our team: There was casting to be done. Who could possibly play the iconic Michael Landon? Locations had to be found. We had to find a home as grand as his was, but it had to be affordable and accessible to our trucks. We had to assemble a crew to cover lighting, camera, wardrobe and hair — experts on the period.

We ended up shooting in San Diego and I had to live out of a hotel room. I stayed on the job and completed it, but very soon the side effects of the cancer drugs made it very difficult for me to stay on my feet all day, to stay conscious. My wonderful husband, Chuck, moved in with me to help me keep steady. My partners, Allen Epstein, Jim Green and Marc Bacino were gracious enough to assign their staff writer, Val McIlroy, to get me through the rewrites. It was touch and go for me, but the team brought the project in on time and it turned out to be a very successful and highly rated movie for the network. Still to this day, I get residuals from its broadcasts in Europe.

A happy ending to the production story. A blessing, yes. But I will never forget the terror or the irony that filled my days as I went for treatment, nor the love and spiritual support I got from the Landons, my own family and beloved medical team at City of Hope in Duarte, California. I found courage where there was little.

Michael Landon prayed for another chance at life. He was not granted one. For some reason, I was. As a result, I take nothing for granted anymore and live every day in gratitude. Now that's lingo I can live with.

"I love a warm pig belly for
my aching feet."

—The Red Queen, *Alice In Wonderland* (2011)

Step Eight.

Build your script one scene after another.
Flashbacks? Research!

There are a number of techniques you can use to write a script. Whichever method suits you best is the right way.

Some writers use 3X5 index cards to develop their scenes. They are your map to the three act paradigm. By literally pinning them to a wall or spreading them out on a floor or table, you can "see" each scene at your fingertips. This will show you how your movie is playing out.

To use the card method begin with your opening. Take a blank card, write the purpose of the scene, the people in it, the location, time, etc. What happens there? How does it advance your story? Then go on to the next one. Step by step, card by card until you come to the ending. Remember, for every action in life there is an equal reaction. Action, reaction. Action, reaction. As in life, your character must act and somebody reacts.

What does your character need? How many obstacles can you throw in front of this need? The answers become scenes and the information goes on the cards.

For example, if I were using the card technique and was coming to the scene I showed you earlier from *Michael Landon, The Father I Knew,* I'd write:

"Scene 60: Michael Sr., his wife Lynn, Leslie, INT. BEVERLY HILLS HOUSE – FOYER — NIGHT. Michael is interrupted by Lynn as he tells Leslie, his daughter, he's fallen in love with another woman. Lynn tells Leslie to go to her room. When she pushes him for answers, Michael tells Lynn the affair he's having is not over but has become a serious relationship. He wants the other woman and he wants Lynn too. Heartbroken, Lynn throws him out."

Instead of cards, some writers, like me, prefer to write treatments or outlines of their story. A treatment is a broad-stroked narrative synopsis of your story with a little dialogue thrown in to establish character. Treatments can be 4-20 pages long.

I usually write an outline when on a deadline because the process helps me to find my story in fewer steps. An outline is an in-depth, detailed look at the story points incorporating a good deal of dialogue and can be up to 60 pages long.

I have also taken three sheets of blank paper, headed Act I, Act II and Act III and made a list of scenes that go in each Act as I figure them out. It's easy to cross out a scene on the list and move it to another act, as easy as dropping one card from an act and moving it to another.

Don't be afraid to change things at this stage. This is the time to spot your story's weaknesses. Better now than after you've written a hundred pages, right? Rearrange the cards looking for stronger conflict and bigger obstacles for your protagonist to hurdle. Never be afraid to up the ante. What have you got to lose?

Hang out with your cards and lists for a week or two before you begin writing. Experiment. Change what you think *should* happen. Surprise your audience and yourself by coming up with something unexpected. It's a valuable part of the process. The cards are just a guide. Challenge them. Can each scene be more dramatic, more touching, more unusual? Don't let the cards have the last word. You're the boss.

There are two techniques to screenwriting. SHOT-BY-SHOT TECHNIQUE or MASTER SCENE TECHNIQUE. Any directors here? Usually writer-director types use the Shot-by-Shot technique. Shot by shot is literally what the camera sees. It's a series of SINGLE CAMERA SHOTS with little or no narrative to explain what's going on.

The Master Scene technique is when all the narrative, action and dialogue is written beneath the initial description of a locale. And you can combine both types of technique in the same script. Look at this example from *Toot-Toot-Tootsie, Goodbye*, a script my co-writer, Martin Tahse, and I adapted from Ron Powers' fabulous novel of the same name. We combined both methods of screenwriting as we cut from the broadcast booth to players on the ball field to show the action. The O.S. behind the character's name means the sound is off-screen, the character is talking but is not seen. When we use V.O., that means voice over which signifies that it will have to be recorded and then edited in later. Very often when there is a voice in an airport, that is always V.O. An actor is hired to record that dialogue in a recording studio and the tape or mp3 file is then delivered to the editor of the picture to include in the final cut or assemblage.

CLOSE ON A SMALL PORTABLE RADIO (*This means a close up.*)

                    L.C. (O.S.)
Top of the ninth, Dodgers 4, Nats 2. Two men on base and it's left-handed rookie Drew Firestone up at bat.

INT. FLUSHING STADIUM - OPENING DAY - LATER

A soft drink vendor sits on a concrete step, cooling his heels and listening to the game.

                    TURTLE (O.S.)
He's fresh from the Ozarks that's brought us some great ones, folks... Paul and Dizzy Dean...Pepper Martin...

HOME PLATE (*This is shot by shot technique when you are literally calling the shot you want the camera to photograph.*)

Drew Firestone, a large red-headed kid, takes a swing at the ball, which smacks into the catcher's mitt.

                    TURTLE (O.S.)
...the wild horse of the Osage who ran out and kissed the earth at home plate before the World Series.

ANNOUNCER'S BOOTH (*The description underneath is the master shot technique of writing.*)

L.C.'s shirt is open under his red blazer, pencil behind his
ear, hair plastered to his head from the heat. Turtle sits
beside him, his shirt crumpled and wet with perspiration.
We are taken by the joy they generate doing what they
love. Nudges, insides, Morse code of alerts and signals.
Behind them is JOEY, thirty-five, their engineer,

                        L.C.
STRIKE ONE...Yessir, and there was Vinegar Bend
Mizell and our own Elvin Ray Watkins ...Firestone
swings again and misses...who's been up here with
me since he hung up his catcher's mask with the
Giants... ball one.
            (takes a pull on his beer)
Turtle learned to snag foul pop ups by catching
hailstones barehanded during a summer
storm....Strike two.

                      TURTLE
You're righter than rain, L.C. Just the way it
happened. Have me a little place down in Fayette,
Arkansas for off- season activity. The Bowl-A-Wile,
in case you're passing through.
            (turns and grins at Joey)
You too, Joey. For those of you who don't know,
Joey's our engineer, a recent addition to the booth.
Well, five years.

                        L.C.
Corey gets the signal. The pitch and...Firestone
connects with the ball! It's a high foul into the air
behind home plate!

L.C., clutching his butterfly net, lunges out of the booth in a comic attempt to catch the foul ball.

CLOSE ON THE STANDS

as the fans jump to their feet to cheer L.C. on.

CLOSE ON A TV CAMERA on the field as it whirls around and trains its eye on L.C.

TV ANNOUNCER BOOTH

L.C. is on the TV monitor, dangling from the booth and dipping toward the ball. Behind him, Turtle exaggeratedly holds L.C. by his belt.

DOWNING (O.S.)
There go our radio boys...go for it, L.C.!

L.C. misses, and the ball drops to the ground.

FANS (O.S.)
(mock disappointment)
OOOOOOOOOH.

JACK DOWNING, the TV announcer, twenty-nine, is immaculately dressed in a blue blazer, white shirt and red tie. He turns to his COLOR MAN, same approximate age, identically dressed.

DOWNING
Old gags only get better sometimes. How long have they been doing that, Bob?

> BOB
>
> Probably back when Jack Benny and Fred Allen
> were making everyone laugh, too.

ANNOUNCER BOOTH

Turtle, playing his part, heroically hoists L.C. back into
the booth, raising his arm in triumph.

BLEACHERS

Fans break into applause and cheers.

ANOTHER ANGLE

Humphries, waiting to go to bat, turns and spits
in disgust.

ANNOUNCER BOOTH

L.C. sits down at his mike. Turtle takes a pull on his beer.

> L.C.
>
> A few more feet on the handle of my net, Turtle,
> and I'd a had that high foul from Firestone.
> Dodgers four, Nats two, two men on base. One and
> two as...Firestone swings and - Criminy! Where are
> the hitters these days? Strike three for the rookie!

> TURTLE
>
> That brings Bogart Humphries up to bat....Talk
> about hitters, this big guy is what the old doc
> ordered.

                         L.C.
        At least what the Nats ordered. Two out, two on
        base. It takes nerves of steel to be standing on that
        plate right now. Cory does his special wind-up...
We hear the CRACK of the bat all the way up in
the booth.

                    L.C. (CONT'D)
        AND THE NEW BOY GETS HOLD OF ONE!

ANOTHER ANGLE

The ball sails through the cloudless blue sky.

ANOTHER ANGLE

Fans leap to their feet and track the ball.

ANOTHER ANGLE

Shoat crosses home plate.

ANNOUNCER BOOTH

L.C. and Turtle are on their feet.

                         L.C.
                  (shouting louder)
        DEWEY BACK BACK BACK....

ANOTHER ANGLE

Dewey doesn't connect with the ball.

CLOSE ON L.C.

                    L.C.
    AND IT'S TOOT-TOOT-TOOTSIE, GOOOOOOD-
    BYE!
ANOTHER ANGLE

Bogart Humphries jogs across home plate.

ANNOUNCER BOOTH

                    L.C.
    AND A BOGART HUMPHRIES BLAST WINS IT
    FOR THE NATS ON OPENING DAY! FINAL
    SCORE - NATS FIVE, DODGERS FOUR!

                  TURTLE
    Who woulda thunk it.

L.C., exhausted from the excitement, coughs into his
handkerchief. Turtle leans into the mike.

                  TURTLE
    Can you believe it, folks?....

NATS DUGOUT

Cha Cha and the other players are shouting, enjoying
their victory. Pachelbel pounds Humphries on the
shoulder.

               TURTLE (O.S.)
    The south's gonna rise again!

With a whoop, Humphries takes a swing at a portable radio on the bench, smashing it into pieces of black vinyl and silencing L.C. and Turtle.

The word "ballpark" reminds me of another story to share. As kids in the 60's, my older brother, Dick McCalla, taught me how to score games listening to the legendary Vin Scully.

He'd show me how to draw the baseball diamond and record the balls and strikes and errors. I loved being close to him without getting punched or teased and I attributed his benevolence to the calm that Vinny's voice always seemed to restore to our chaotic household.

In my mind, Vinny bonded us as secret friends. He was Dick's hero, and now he was mine.

Fast forward to 30 years later. I had arranged for Martin and me to sit with the great Vinny to research "Tootsie". My heart raced as we took the elevator to the broadcast booth. I about melted when I saw the view that inspired him to draw the voice pictures that transported radio fans to the park and beyond.

For me, Vinny WAS the character of L.C. Fanning, a master story-teller able to give us nuanced verbal histories on every player. With a brilliant turn of phrase, he could take us to the player's home towns, to where their mothers made apple pie, to where they first threw that slider and how, with hard work and spit, they became true boys of summer. When Vinny called a game, you could smell that pie.

Vinny made me so comfortable that I told him the story I just told you. "My brother would never believe this." I whispered. Vinny grinned and said. "Well, let's get him on the phone."

My hands shook as I dialed, praying Dick was at home to talk to his hero. I could barely contain myself when I heard his familiar "Lo." and blurted out, "You'll never guess where

I am sitting!" When I told him I was at Dodger Stadium in Vinny's booth, there was a long silence then a skeptical. "What?!" I handed the phone to Vinny who was sitting so close I could smell a hint of dry cleaning fluid wafting from his sports jacket. "Hi there, Richard!" Scully chirped in that unmistakable baritone. I could hear the recognition in Dick's, "Oh my gosh! It is you." For a few delightful minutes, the two men chatted about baseball and the leagues. More than just a telephone conversation, it was another full circle moment for me.

Finally, in my brother's eyes, I was more than a kid sister. Now, sealed in the sanctity of the announcer's booth and the magic of Nancy Bea Heffley, the organ lady not fifteen feet away, I was someone to be reckoned with. I was an authentic girl of summer on a night that ended far too soon.

Remember, your job is to write the script, not tell the director how to shoot it. A sign of an amateur is a preponderance of camera angles. Don't use them unless you cannot convey what you mean any other way. In the sequence you just read, we had to use angles to show the reaction of and the relative distance of all the players in a large space like a ball park.

If you decide your epic begins in childhood and you're considering doing a cradle-to-grave piece, be careful not to spend too much time with the child character. Audiences may not want to get involved with the adult if the child takes too much of their focus early on. A perfect example of this is *Cinema Paradiso.* A wonderful film, but if you remember, we fell in love with the boy and out of love with him as a man. There's a rule of thumb that says changing an actor in the first act seems to work best, so if you want to do a slice of life about your childhood, either stay in childhood the whole piece or move to adulthood in twenty minutes of a TV movie or the first half hour of a feature.

A perfect example of this is *Beyond the Sea*. In the Bobby Darin story, we saw young Bobby as a sick kid with rheumatic fever for about ten minutes. Then the script jumped to show him as young adult played by Kevin Spacey.

Everyone likes to say flashbacks are passé and writers only use them when they're in trouble. Don't tell the writer of *Amadeus* or *The Notebook*, *Bridges of Madison County*, *Ray* or *The Martian*.

HOW DO YOU WRITE A FLASHBACK?

Let's say you want to tell a story about your childhood from an adult point of view. Point of view means the way you see the story. You would introduce yourself as the adult at the beginning and go back in time to tell your story.

In *The Notebook*, the present frame is James Garner's character reading Gena Rowland's character's diary to her, hoping it will pull her back from Alzheimer's. As he reads to her, we go back in time to see the words in the book come to life.

In *Amadeus*, Salieri, the court composer ridden with guilt for driving Mozart crazy, attempts suicide and tells his story in flashback to a priest.

China's Pearl, is a script that I wrote for the stellar actress and human being, Valerie Harper (*Rhoda*, *The Mary Tyler Moore Show*, *Blame it on Rio*) and her kind and clever husband, film and Broadway producer Tony Cacciotti (*The Dragon and the Pearl*, *Golda's Balcony*, *Looped*). The script was about the author, Pearl S. Buck and her amazing life, told in flashback. I introduced Pearl in her eighties having to make a decision as to whether or not to give an interview to the press after forty years of being abused by them. While she mulls it over, I take the audience into her head and her memories. By the time she decides to talk to them near the end of the story, we've seen all that the media did to her and understand why it is such a hard decision for her to make. Opening and closing a film in this manner is often called "bookending."

On a personal note, after I finished the script, I produced a 24-hour American Cancer Walk For Life with my friend Nigel Crook in West Hollywood. The point was to enroll volunteers to walk for 24 hours straight to raise money to fight cancer. Not only did Valerie offer to be our Mistress of Ceremonies, but Tony asked me when I had the least amount of support and he and their daughter, Cristina, showed up at 2 AM to walk! These are kindnesses I'll never forget.

I used bookends on another movie that I wrote and produced for Peter Guber's Mandalay Films. That film was *Get to the Heart: The Barbara Mandrell Story* based on Barbara's memoir of the same name and directed by my good friend, the inventive and prolific, Jerry London (*Shogun, Ellis Island, Chiefs*).

I opened the story with the multi-talented Barbara Mandrell in her forties about to begin a live concert in California. A slight case of nerves keeps her from going on stage. Her friend, Dolly Parton, reminds her how much courage she has shown in life. Those memories – from her beginnings as a child performer through her survival of a terrible automobile crash – are the basis of the film. We end the flash back in the wings of that same concert as Barbara, with fears assuaged, steps out and wows the audience with her confidence and powerful voice.

Mentioning Barbara reminds me of the importance and fun of doing research and collecting source material. Barbara, played wonderfully by the talented Maureen McCormick (*The Brady Bunch, Teen Angel*), spent most of her life on the road traveling with her family from town to town. As part of my research, I got to go on the road with Barbara in her deluxe tour bus from her home outside of Nashville to Branson, Missouri.

She and I talked through the night as her husband and manager, Ken Dudney (played by actor Greg Kean in the film), slept in the bus' master bedroom. She told me that as a child of the road, she never got to go to dances at school. She recounted how she stopped the bus one night and via walkie talkie, invited her band members off their bus to come play dance music. I was so enamored with the idea of her staging a dance party in a bus that she had the drivers pull the two busses over to the side of the road and she re-created the moment for me!

There we were, two lucky ladies surrounded by a bevy of male musicians, heading down the highway at sixty miles an hour across the state of Tennessee, dancing the night away. Barbara and Ken were such fun and great to work with. A couple with a deep Christain faith, they made me feel at home in their lives and remain two of the finest people I have ever met.

Flashbacks get a bad rap but it's amazing just how much they're still used. It's up to you if you want to use them within the story. But remember, with flashbacks you still need a clear beginning, middle and end.

How do you research your own or another's life story? Where do you get the material for your screenplay about yourself or anyone else? From source material. What is source material?

Source material is the facts and details you find to supplement your story. You can get source material from:

1. memories
2. a book
3. a play
4. the internet
5. interviews
6. television and radio programs
7. an article in a magazine or newspaper
8. a diary or journal
9. word of mouth

For more than twenty-three movies, and my television episodic work, I read all printed material on the subjects. In a true story, I interviewed my protagonists and every willing person who knew them, using an audio recorder to get the facts straight. You must get permission ahead of time to use a recorder, but most people are fine with it. Recordings can act also as a back up if anyone decides to change their mind after stating their facts.

From the interviews, I got the good the bad and the ugly in each of my protagonist's lives. I would often end up with hours of interviews. It's a lot of material to sift through and it cost me to pay someone else to transcribe the recordings, but the information was invaluable. I got the characters' voices, their rhythm of speaking, their true feelings. This proves to be so much better than making it up! Which reminds me of another story.

I was hired by ABC and Jaffe/ Braunstein Films to write the story of a group of women incarcerated in a Georgia prison for petty crimes. They were allegedly being abused and had found a lawyer to represent them in a class action suit against the state. The women claimed they were forced to dress up as prostitutes at night then were sexually assaulted by certain guards, the warden and, on occasion, even the Governor himself and his friends.

When I asked for permission to go inside the prison to interview these ladies, the first response from the new female warden was "No!" I told her that I had already heard the allegations and if she didn't let me in to see for myself, I would have to make it up based on what I was told by the inmates alone. Wanting her new regime to look sparkling clean, she weighed the options and finally allowed me to visit.

When the large iron door slammed behind me, chills shot up my spine. I saw a sign that read, "We Shoot Through

Hostages." which meant they would shoot through me if anyone decided to take me as a hostage. What had I gotten myself
into? Could any movie be worth the risk of being shot? At that
moment, I wanted to back out. Instead, I allowed myself to be
escorted by the new warden from one area of the prison to
another. I received cat calls and looks from the inmates that
shook me to my core.

Unfortunately, many of the women I was to interview were
mentally ill. As the warden escorted me into their isolated
ward, they followed me like I was the pied piper, pulling at my
clothes and touching my hair. Their stories touched me. I knew
this was the only chance they would ever get to make any
real money and to set the record straight, so I persevered.
I had to do justice to the story and to the real women involved.

The movie starring Judith Light (*Who's the Boss,
Transparent*) and Stacy Keach (*American History X, Titus*) did
well on American television and is shown still in Europe as a
feature film called *Against Their Will: Women in Prison*.

Even if it's your own life, you still need to do research.
You need to discover how others see you. What do they
remember? What was their take on the events you're writing
about? How has your life changed theirs, or vice versa?

Pick up the phone. Hit the internet. What happened in the
world during the time frame of your story? What were the
headlines? Not only will these headlines inspire and inform
you, they may feed your subplots.

Was there a war going on? The Great Depression? Was it
before or after the computer revolution? Was it baseball
season? Was a newsworthy trial going on? How about an inter-
national intrigue? Was the weather unusual? The answers to
these questions will also supply you with your subplots.

Can you play your story against history? One of the most
famous movies that did so was *Gone with the Wind*. A small love

story in all respects, set against a huge canvas of the Civil War. Do you remember other smaller stories played against a larger event? How about *The Bridge on the River Kwai, The Deerhunter, Cold Mountain, Dr. Zhivago*? These are films where large worldly circumstances become characters in the film.

Doing research is fun and integral to any true or fictional story. If you don't use the material, at least it will have expanded your own mind. Get more information than you need. There's nothing worse than flying for thirty pages and then coming to a screeching halt because you've literally run out of things to write about.

"I'll sleep with you for a meatball."

—Julie Andrews, *Victor/Victoria* (1982)

Step Nine.

Be a Legal Beagle. Dot your I's, cross your T's and get the rights!

Once you've decided on your story, ask yourself, who's involved besides you? If a person in your movie is a celebrity, and you don't defame them or invade their right to privacy, their lives are considered public domain and can be written about. But if you write about everyday friends or family, and they are totally recognizable as themselves in the piece, best to get written permission up front.

If you sell the script, the studio or network will insist on written permissions that they structure. If you've finished your movie about Uncle Fred without permission and sold it and Uncle Fred says no, you've worked hard for naught and look like an amateur to the studio execs. Better to share your vision of how your characters fit into the story with the real people you're writing about and get their OK. Tell the truth and don't make promises you can't keep.

Many years ago, I was asked by my talent agency, Creative Artists Agency, to develop a TV movie for the ex-wife of a major movie star. The ex told me she had found a true story in San Diego, California and was very excited about me writing it for her to produce.

I made my first call to the proposed subject of the piece and was surprised at how nasty she was to me. After being verbally abused for about twenty minutes, I discovered the star's ex-wife had not gotten the rights nor her permission and in no way did the woman want a movie written about her life. Needless to say, I had assumed the ex was a professional and had taken care of the details. I was wrong. Learn to cover your own behind in this business and don't assume anything.

Listen to what Jesse Salvar and Matt Galsor of *Legal Ease* have to say about life rights in their Q and A blog for "Film Independent." (http://www/filmindependent.org):

"Q: I have a question that I've been toiling over for months. I've done some research on it and cannot find a clear answer. I'm beginning to work with a writer on a screenplay on someone who died about 20 years ago. She has surviving brothers, but her parents are dead and she never married or had children. What type of life story rights do we need to acquire to tell this story - a screenplay that could potentially turn into a feature film? I guess the first question should be do I even need to buy or acquire the life story rights? Can I just change her name?

A: First of all, there is really no such thing as life story rights. There is only the right against being defamed. There is the right against certain private facts about you being publicly disclosed without your permission - the New York Times would be violating it if its reporter sneaked in your bedroom, copied your most secret diary entries, and published them. And there are certain other rights of this nature. But there are no life story rights. When you buy life story rights, what you really "buy" is a promise from the subject of your story that they will not sue you for defamation or any number of other possible violations of their privacy rights.

In theory, you can make a movie about anyone alive without obtaining their life story rights, as long as the movie doesn't defame the subject and doesn't violate all these other privacy rights. In practice, that's hard to do and no matter how much you try not to violate these rights, you can't stop someone from alleging you did. So practically, in most cases, when a movie is made about someone alive, life story rights.

And here's what they say about defaming the dead:

Jun 15, 2009

Q: *I have recently optioned the autobiography of a person that I'd like to use as the subject for a feature film. In the last quarter of the book, a historical figure whom my subject served with in the military is featured in a number of scenes. Do I have to get clearance from the person's estate before using them in the script? I assume the author got permission to use her story in his book, but does this permission extend to a film?* **A:** *Judging by your question, I think I can assume that your historical figure is truly historic (i.e., he or she is history). Either that or you are pondering getting clearance from someone's large house. I'll assume the former. The fact that your person of interest is an historic figure and is no longer with us makes your question much easier to answer.*

Whenever you're depicting real people in a film, there are three main things you need to worry about: defamation, right of publicity and right of privacy. Because of the facts in your situation, you may be able to imitate Alfred E. Neuman and sit back, smile and ask "What, Me Worry?"

With respect to defamation, the historical figure's family's loss is your gain (sorry about that, historical figure's family). As a rule, you cannot defame the dead. Under the law, the right to not be defamed is a personal right – only the person in question can sue for defamation. Therefore, a family member cannot bring a claim against you. I'm assuming you're going to try to recreate reality the best you can but even if you decide to portray the person as a raving lunatic, that person can't sue you for defamation because that person can't do much of anything considering their physical state.

When it comes to right of publicity, it doesn't matter that your historic figure is deceased because family members do have a continuing right to prevent others from using their dead loved one's name and likeness for commercial purposes (which triggers a right of publicity). Additionally, this right applies to both public and private figures. Therefore, this could be a concern. The good news, however, is that use of a person's name and likeness in a film has been held not to be the type of use that violates a right of publicity. Although your film will hopefully make money, courts have held that they are more akin to art than a commercial product. Please note, however, that if your movie is the next summer's blockbuster, you cannot include depictions of this real person on any merchandising, commercial tie-ins or the like, because that may be considered a violation of that person's right of publicity that can be actionable by the person's family. In other words, I don't want to see a McDonald's Happy Meal action figure depicting your historical figure (actually, as a consumer, I'd love to see it – but as your legal conscience, I don't).

That leaves rights of privacy. This is a fairly complex area of law. Luckily, and without even getting into whether or *not the historical figure's family could have a claim against you on such grounds, by your use of the term "historical figure," I'm assuming he or she was a public figure. A public figure has significant hurdles to jump over in order to have a valid claim of an invasion of their right of privacy. Due to the fact that it sounds like you're depicting something that could be in the public interest, without knowing all the facts, I would think your first amendment right should keep you safe.*

From the answer above, you can see that it likely doesn't matter whether the author of the autobiography acquired the film rights to this historical figure's life. Most likely the author did not and did not need to for the reasons referenced above.

If you're thinking about doing an adaptation of a book or other written source, you need to option the material. Having an option means you have the sole right to develop the material for a specific period of time. The idea is to get a contract for the longest period of time for the least amount of money.

It can take a long time to get a project written and sold. Make sure you have a year at the very least and the right to extend it should you need more time. Options can cost from $1 to hundreds of thousands of dollars. If you play your cards right, they can be free. Paying a buck by check is better though because in some states you need a written record of a cash exchange to protect your rights. You would include the check with a letter of intent. (See example on the next page.)

You don't need a lawyer up front, but you do need a letter of agreement signed by both you and the person whose material you are optioning. The method I use is to call the person and get a verbal agreement as to how much I am going to pay and what they might get from a studio or production company should a sale be concluded. I tell them I need a year at least and two years at best. Then I send them a written agreement. The letter might go something like this:

March 1, 2016,

Dear Mrs. Smith,

As we discussed on the phone, this is a letter of agreement signifying my right to develop your article for *Ms. Magazine* titled "Bring on the Big Guns" into a film.

    For the sum of $1.00, you grant me the sole rights to develop and sell my screenplay based on said article to a third party, expiring on _____. Upon that date, I have the right to re-up my option for a second two years if I need the extra time.

    Should my efforts result in a sale, you agree to negotiate in good faith separately with the producers for the buyout of your material, not to exceed $_____.

    Please sign both copies of this letter and return one to me in the enclosed self-addressed stamped envelope.

Linda Bergman _____, Dated_____

Mrs. Smith_____, Dated_____

Check # 1234 attached

Whether you use a lawyer or not, it's cleaner and safer to have all legal work done up front. If you do use a letter of agreement, it protects you. But know that if a studio or network buys your script, they'll insist on their own contracts written by their lawyer and countered by yours. A lawyer might take ten to fifteen percent of your salary or he'll want an hourly wage, usually in the hundreds per hour. There are a number of entertainment lawyers listed online and listed in the many reference books on Hollywood. It's better to meet with them in person if possible to decide if you are simpatico and if their fees agree with your budget. In a pinch, you can always have a phone conversation. Take careful notes and write a follow up note to the lawyer to cement the numbers mentioned in the conversation.

Take a look at the website, "Done Deal Pro" (www.donedealpro.com). They offer examples for all kinds of deals, i.e., disclosure agreements, literary agent agreements, agency packaging agreement, release forms, life rights option agreement, etc. They have generously allowed me to print their glossary of industry terms that you can find at the end of this chapter.

Be respectful of what you ask and grateful for what you get back when you send your script out. Because of the volume of material all agents receive, most likely you will not get a response unless the agent is interested in the material. It may not be fair nor polite but it is the way it works.

DONE DEAL PRO'S
www.donedealpro.com

Glossary of Industry Terms

Here is a list of terms related to writing, as well as terms and phrases you will encounter working with and in the industry as a writer.

against - used in reference to payment for a script or property. A sum of money is initially paid up front as a down payment towards a final and total sum of money. The difference between the two dollar amounts is paid at a later date which is determined in the contract in advance. That date could be once the script is finished being written, or after a rewrite is done or a polish, or even at the beginning or ending of the filming of the screenplay (production of the film).

attached - when actor, director or producer has agreed to be in a film or involved with it. In most cases they are contractually tied to the property.

backdoor pilot - an episode is taped/filmed as a stand alone TV movie (story), so it still can be broadcast even if it is not picked up as a series.

bare bones pilot - an episode is produced on a small budget and contains no real special effects, and features a condensed story. This allows the producers and writers to show off the style and general mood of the show and thus hopeful convince the network to pay for a more polished version that can be aired.

beat sheet - a breakdown of the key moments/scenes in a film. Lists the highlights and key scenes of the entire script or story.

consider - a somewhat favorable response from a reader which is usually noted on the coverage they do on a script or treatment. It is not a guarantee that the material will be passed on to the next level. It usually represents more of an ambivalence on the reader's part. Not a pass but not a strong recommendation that it be read either.

coverage - a reader's report on a script which is generally comprised of three parts. The first page is generally the most basic of information on the material: title, who wrote it, genre, date, draft, time period, who submitted to, who submitted by, etc.. The report also consists of a synopsis of the script which is usually a one page to two page description of the story (or events that take place in the script). And the last part of the report involves comments by the reader on what elements if any they liked and or disliked about the script's story, characters, writing, originality, etc.

creative exec - an individual that reviews literary material to determine whether a studio or company, etc. is interested in optioning or purchasing it. This person is usually next in line after a reader. They also will generally help to oversee the further development of a project once it is optioned or purchased providing the writer with feedback, suggestions, and changes for rewrites.

dialogue pass - when a writer focuses only on rewriting or "polishing" the dialogue in a draft of a script.

development - the process during which a story or idea is written and formed into a script or a completed script is rewritten further to create a script ready to be produced.

development hell - when the process of writing or rewriting a script continues over a long period of time. This usually involves numerous notes and rewrites along with frequently contradicting directions given by the various participants.

feature - a full length movie, usually ranging in length from 90 minutes to 120 minutes.

first look deal - an arrangement either a company or in some cases an individual has with a studio, in which they must allow the studio the first right of refusal on purchasing and or producing a project the individual or company is interested in. If the studio passes, the project can then be "shopped" around to other interested parties.

green light - when a script and thus a film gets the final approval from, in most cases, a studio to proceed with making the project. This is usually given once a final budget is approved, though sometimes the rewrite of a script might affect this along with a certain actor or actress agreeing to be in the project.

heat - when a project/script generates a great deal of interest from the filmmaking community. This generally leads to high sale price for the material as companies and studios attempt to outbid one another for the rights. An individual can also be in high demand based on the selling success of their projects or a recently produced project.

high concept - refers to an idea that sounds very commercially appealing and in many cases unique and original. Usually associated with big blockbuster films but can reference any idea or script that would appear to have great potential.

indie - short for independent. Can refer to a film or production company that works outside of the Hollywood/studio system.

log line - short one sentence description of the story in a script or book or for an idea.

MOW - stands for Movie of the Week. Refers to feature length films that are made just for showing on television (network).

notes - feedback and comments on a creative property. Can consist of changes, suggestions of tone, mood, etc.

option - a studio, production company, and or producer pays a someone for the exclusive rights to a literary property for a set amount of time. At the end of the time period, the material can, in most cases be optioned again, but if not, the rights revert back the original owner (or writer).
outline - a scene by scene breakdown/list of the story of a script. Shows each point and beat.

package - the collection of talent and material that is put together by an agent or agency in which a script is tied together with certain actors, actresses, and or directors and producers. This usually increases the chance of selling the property to a studio.

page one (rewrite) - a complete re-write of a script in which a major portion of the script is altered including the plot, scene order, character types, theme, etc. This can be done by the original writer or by a screenwriter brought in to totally redo the screenplay.

pass - a rejection from a studio, company, agent, etc. It can also refer to a writer rewriting certain elements of script including dialogue, character, action, etc.

pilot - a test episode of an intended or potential television series. They will usually set the general background and tell the origin story for the series.

pitch - to verbally/orally describe the story of a script or idea.

polish - when a writer rewrites certain aspects of the script. Major changes are generally not made at all. This usually involves changing some dialogue, refining a character arc or action, etc.

property - a script, book, or other literary material.

put pilot - when a deal is made to produce a pilot that includes heavy penalties if the pilot is not aired. This is virtually a guarantee that a pilot will be picked up.

query (letter) - a written request to see if a producer, agent, manager, studio, etc. would be interested in "looking at" a script, treatment, or story idea.

reader - a person hired by a production company, producer, director, studio, or agent to read a script then write coverage on it. They generally work free lance and are paid approximately $45 a script.

recommend - a very favorable response from a reader which is noted on the coverage they do on a script or treatment. It is not a guarantee that the material will be bought, but it represents getting by the "first line of defense." In most cases this means the script will either be verbally discussed in a meeting or passed on to the next level for consideration by a development executive, or by an agent or producer.

signatory - a studio or company that is officially a member of the Screen Actors Guild, the Writers Guild and or the Directors Guild and have agreed to their terms.

sitcom - shorthand for a half hour situation comedy television series.

solicited - when a script or project is requested for review by a studio, company or agent from a writer, agent, manager and or producer.

spec - a script that was written without the prior guarantee that it would be sold. In other words, it was written with the speculation that it might sell. Most scripts written are considered "speculative."

synopsis - a brief, usually one half to two page description of a story or plot. Written in prose form generally with little to no dialogue.

take a meeting - this generally refers to one individual meeting with another. In can also refer to an individual being the center of a discussion and thus leading the direction and pace of it.

telefilm - feature-length motion picture made for television. (Also see MOW.)

track - to follow the development of a project even if it is not owned by the individual watching its progress.

trade (trade papers) - daily periodicals which report on the latest news and events in the film business. The two most popular being the Hollywood Reporter and Variety.

treatment - similar in form and style to a synopsis but only a much more detailed telling of a story. Generally includes every scene and plot involved. These are also written in a prose form, similar to a novel, but still usually with little to no dialogue. They are considered more or less a tool for writers when they are initially fleshing out their idea(s) for script.

turnaround - after a certain period of time, if a project/script is not produced, a studio or company will essentially offer the script to any buyers interested in acquiring the rights to it. This usually involves the other company or individual paying for all "expenses" incurred while the project was being developed. These are fees and expenses that were on top on the purchase price for the material. Due to the high cost of development this can cause the project to then be very expensive and thus less attractive.

unsolicited - a script or project that is sent to a company, studio, and or individual that was not requested before it was sent — either in writing or by phone.

*"Are you crazy? The fall will
probably kill you."*

—Butch Cassidy, *Butch Cassidy and the Sundance Kid* (1969)

Step Ten.

How To Get It Out There and
Protect Your Work

First copyright your script. Many people think if they simply register it with the Writers Guild (WGA) that their script is protected. But that is not good enough.

Art Buchwald infamously fought the good fight against Paramount. He won a judgment against them after they lifted his script idea and turned it into *Coming to America*.

The decision was important mainly for the court's determination of damages resulting from Paramount's "unconscionable" means of determining how much to pay authors. Fearing a loss if it appealed, and the subsequent implications of the decision across all its other contracts, Paramount settled for undisclosed terms. The case was the subject of a 1992 book, *Fatal Subtraction: The Inside Story of Buchwald v. Paramount* by Pierce O'Donnell, the lawyer who represented Buchwald, and *Los Angeles Times* reporter Dennis McDougal.

Even if you are in the working stages of your script, if you are going to expose your material, it's good to copyright it. Here's the latest advice on that from *EHow.com:*

> "There have been a growing number of lawsuits in which movie screenplays have been "stolen." Writers devote themselves to finishing a script or screenplay and before they can get their work professionally seen, a movie begins production and the characters and plot are unbelievably similar to the writer's work. To protect yourself against movie script piracy, you can be protected by copyright under the category of Performing Art Works.
>
> Your work can be protected from the moment of creation without the requirement of actually registering your copyrighted movie script. However, **ALWAYS** officially copyright your work with the government office in charge of copyrights.
>
> In the United States, the government office in charge of copyrights is the Library of Congress (http://copyright.gov/)."

After you've protected your work, you want to put it out there. To get an agent, start by writing what is called a query letter that includes professional facts about you and a description of your screenplay.

Don't try to be clever or cute. Most agents have heard it all. Be direct and professional. The purpose of the letter is to get the person receiving it to request a copy of the entire script. The letter should be one page long or shorter. ONE PAGE!

A good way to open the letter is with your script's logline. A one or two sentence grabber, i.e. "*Not Dead Yet* is a romantic comedy about a reality show producer and what happens when the ghost of his fiancée returns to haunt him on set."

Introduce yourself and your writing credits if any. If you don't have any credits you can list whatever credentials you have that are pertinent to the script you're pitching. If your script is a police drama and you were a cop mention that in your letter. It adds credibility to your project. If your script is funny and you're currently a member of a local improv group, say so. Use whatever credits you have no matter how small they might be. Don't underestimate yourself. Did you work as a journalist for a few years? That's professional writing experience. Did you win an award in college for a short play you wrote? That's worth mentioning. Did you earn an MFA? That might be impressive to a producer. There's usually a reason why you wrote a script which gives you some extra credibility and you should think about that and try and tie that in with your writing credentials for the script you're pitching.

Then in your most descriptive, efficient way, tell the story in one or two short paragraphs, i.e:

"Noah (30), a wiz in reality programming has those boy/man looks that women love but don't know why. When his fiancée, Sarah (26), accidentally drowns in their swimming pool, he keeps the tragedy to himself and buries himself in work developing new shows. His nemesis at the mega-mansion that is the show's exotic set is the boss' daughter; gorgeous, spoiled Gracie (26), who is interning for the company. She has set her sights on Noah and is determined to seduce him. All hell breaks loose when Sarah's ghost returns to haunt him. Torn between two women: one in this world, and one in another, Noah struggles to keep his job and tell the truth about what he really wants."

Make sure to include the date of your letter/email and your contact information and end with a thank you.

In the meantime, show the script to friends and family who have access to agents, actors/producers/directors. If your friend likes it, hey, he or she might give you a well-deserved leg up. It is a huge favor to ask someone to take the time to read your masterpiece. Be respectful of what you ask and grateful for what you get.

Here are some excellent recent tips from www.Ehow.com.

"1. Get an agent. This is the most efficient way to sell your script. Do not pay your agent unless you get paid. Many people find first time sellers easy prey and charge them ridiculous and unnecessary fees.

2. Submit your work to competitions. The winner usually gets their script represented and eventually sold. Even if you don't take first place you get great exposure in such events.

One of the judges may really like your work and recommend you to someone who knows somebody.

3. Get a Hollywood Screenwriting Directory. It usually runs around $30, but it is a great tool. It has listings for major studios, executives, producers. It's a great way to find out who to send your query letter to. But call first. People in these jobs change positions frequently.

H O W   D O   I   G E T   A N   A G E N T ?

This is *the* question every student asks. First of all, make sure your material is in tip top shape. Have everyone you know read it and look for typos and ask questions. Secondly, learn to write a good query letter. If you're new to the business, I would advise you to get a job in the industry, even if it is as a Temp doing office work.

For his take, I went to my friend and colleague, Marc Pariser, former William Morris and Creative Artists Agency agent and CEO/Founder of ShowBizCentral.com, the revolutionary new online and mobile platform for people who work in film, television, and digital media. Marc says:

"For those interested in a career in film, television, and digital media as a writer, director, actor or producer, getting representation is essential at some point as early in their career as possible. Unfortunately, most people find getting signed by an agent or manager a mysterious and frustrating process.

Most instruction on this subject that is available will tell you how to properly construct a query letter, tell you how to properly format your script, how long your demo or sizzle reel should be, and impress upon you the importance of networking. Of course these things are important, but, ultimately, not enough.

Here are five important keys to finding and getting representation:

1. **Be ready before approaching an agent.** Most people are so motivated by their belief in their talent and their enthusiasm to launch their career that they approach agents too early. One needs to properly and adequately

develop their craft, assemble some credits and experience, and develop good samples of their work so that agents and managers can effectively and credibly present them to buyers (casting directors, producers, hiring executives at studios, production companies, networks, cable companies, etc.). Do the work to prove yourself before attempting to get an agent.

2. Ask the right questions. Don't be in a hurry to convince people to read your script or look at your reel. Build rapport before asking for something for yourself. Ask them what kind of clients they are looking for, if any...what qualities and credentials they are interested in before they'll consider a new client. Ask them about their own career, and ask for advice. Ask everyone you meet who they would be willing to introduce you to.

3. Decide whether you want an agent or manager, or both. While there is a lot of overlap in what agents and managers do, there are also some distinct differences. Traditionally it was common for actors to have both a manager and an agent. These days it is increasingly common for writers and directors to have both as well. A manager can help get you to the right agent. Agents can introduce you to managers, but won't be eager to do so. Technically agents are tasked with finding employment for their clients, while managers take a more career management approach...but in actuality they both tend to address all the needs of the client and good managers and agents work effectively together as a team.

4. Big agency or small agency? While it's true that the big agencies have the advantage of a wealth of information about what's going on in the marketplace, the most important thing is who is going to work the hardest for you. That means that the individual who represents you is more important than the agency. Finding the right individual at a reputable agency should be the goal. There are plenty of small and mid-size agencies who do a great job for their clients, and there are junior agents at the big agencies who do not yet represent stars who are hungrier and will work harder for you than the senior agents.

5. It's a team effort! Once you've been signed by an agent or manager or both, do not sit by the phone waiting for calls about jobs, submissions, and auditions. Continue to market yourself, continue to network, help your representative help you by sharing information, promoting yourself, telling your reps who you've met at a party so they can follow up. Too many people keep their activities secret while they wait for their representatives to "prove themselves and earn their commission". This attitude is a big mistake. Become a working team with your representatives and you'll both be more successful.

Of course there are other things you can do to facilitate getting signed by an agent or manager. The important thing is to keep working and developing your craft.

If you are a writer, write. If you are an actor, then act. Your goal should be to get inside the business to gain experience, credits, relationships, and be available for opportunities. There are lots of productions happening all the time...everything from web productions to student films, to independent film projects, commercials, industrials, etc. Every production can use an extra set of hands. If there is no job available, then volunteer to help out in any way that you can. Any job on a set, even working in craft services, gets you closer to people with whom you can work and collaborate in the future and who can make introductions and open doors for you. It's important to be on active sets as often as possible to meet the people who are already working…and mainstream creatives often work on indie films in between studio jobs.

The entertainment business is a tough one to break into, yet every year people succeed in getting their foot in the door and launching their careers. You can do it too! Get started by getting to work on your own behalf before you get an agent or manager, and before you get into a guild or union.

The above articles didn't mention this, but practice is the key to getting good at anything and writing a script is no exception. Get into a class or join a writing group to keep you motivated. You may not sell your first script or your second or even your third, but keep them handy and once you get your first break, bring them out again and watch them become invaluable.

Most importantly, don't give up on your dream. Keep writing. And, hopefully, we'll see you "in the movies"!

WGA GREATEST MOVIES LIST

Thanks to the WGA for giving me permission to list their *101 Greatest Screenplays*. This list was created by WGA writers themselves who put the titles to a vote.

1. **CASABLANCA** Screenplay by Julius J. & Philip G. Epstein and Howard Koch. Based on the play "Everybody Comes to Rick's" by Murray Burnett and Joan Alison

2. **THE GODFATHER** Screenplay by Mario Puzo and Francis Ford Coppola. Based on the novel by Mario Puzo

3. **CHINATOWN** Written by Robert Towne

4. **CITIZEN KANE** Written by Herman Mankiewicz and Orson Welles

5. **ALL ABOUT EVE** Screenplay by Joseph L. Mankiewicz. Based on "The Wisdom of Eve," a short story and radio play by Mary Orr

6. **ANNIE HALL** Written by Woody Allen and Marshall Brickman

7. **SUNSET BLVD.** Written by Charles Brackett & Billy Wilder and D.M. Marshman, Jr.

8. **NETWORK** Written by Paddy Chayefsky

9. SOME LIKE IT HOT Screenplay by Billy Wilder & I.A.L. Diamond. Based on "Fanfare of Love," a German film written by Robert Thoeren and M. Logan

10. THE GODFATHER II Screenplay by Francis Ford Coppola and Mario Puzo. Based on Mario Puzo's novel "The Godfather"

11. BUTCH CASSIDY AND THE SUNDANCE KID Written by William Goldman

12. DR. STRANGELOVE Screenplay by Stanley Kubrick and Peter George and Terry Southern. Based on novel "Red Alert" by Peter George

13. THE GRADUATE Screenplay by Calder Willingham and Buck Henry. Based on the novel by Charles Webb

14. LAWRENCE OF ARABIA Screenplay by Robert Bolt and Michael Wilson. Based on the life and writings of Col. T.E. Lawrence

15. THE APARTMENT Written by Billy Wilder & I.A.L. Diamond

16. PULP FICTION Written by Quentin Tarantino. Stories by Quentin Tarantino & Roger Avary

17. TOOTSIE Screenplay by Larry Gelbart and Murray Schisgal. Story by Don McGuire and Larry Gelbart

18. ON THE WATERFRONT Screen Story and Screenplay by Budd Schulberg. Based on "Crime on the Waterfront" articles by Malcolm Johnson

19. TO KILL A MOCKINGBIRD Screenplay by Horton Foote. Based on the novel by Harper Lee

20. IT'S A WONDERFUL LIFE Screenplay by Frances Goodrich & Albert Hackett & Frank Capra. Based on short story "The Greatest Gift" by Philip Van Doren Stern. Contributions to screenplay Michael Wilson and Jo Swerling

21. NORTH BY NORTHWEST Written by Ernest Lehman

22. THE SHAWSHANK REDEMPTION Screenplay by Frank Darabont. Based on the short story "Rita Hayworth and the Shawshank Redemption" by Stephen King

23. GONE WITH THE WIND Screenplay by Sidney Howard. Based on the novel by Margaret Mitchell

24. ETERNAL SUNSHINE OF THE SPOTLESS MIND Screenplay by Charlie Kaufman. Story by Charlie Kaufman & Michel Gondry & Pierre Bismuth

25. THE WIZARD OF OZ Screenplay by Noel Langley and Florence Ryerson and Edgar Allan Woolf Adaptation by Noel Langley. Based on the novel by L. Frank Baum

26. DOUBLE INDEMNITY Screenplay by Billy Wilder and Raymond Chandler. Based on the novel by James M. Cain

27. GROUNDHOG DAY Screenplay by Danny Rubin and Harold Ramis. Story by Danny Rubin

28. SHAKESPEARE IN LOVE Written by Marc Norman and Tom Stoppard

29. SULLIVAN'S TRAVELS Written by Preston Sturges

30. UNFORGIVEN Written by David Webb Peoples

31. HIS GIRL FRIDAY Screenplay by Charles Lederer. Based on the play "The Front Page" by Ben Hecht & Charles MacArthur

32. FARGO Written by Joel Coen & Ethan Coen

33. THE THIRD MAN Screenplay by Graham Greene. Story by Graham Greene. Based on the short story by Graham Greene

34. THE SWEET SMELL OF SUCCESS Screenplay by Clifford Odets and Ernest Lehman. From a novelette by Ernest Lehman

35. THE USUAL SUSPECTS Written by Christopher McQuarrie

36. MIDNIGHT COWBOY Screenplay by Waldo Salt. Based on the novel by James Leo Herlihy

37. THE PHILADELPHIA STORY Screenplay by Donald Ogden Stewart. Based on the play by Philip Barry

38. AMERICAN BEAUTY Written by Alan Ball

39. THE STING Written by David S. Ward

40. WHEN HARRY MET SALLY Written by Nora Ephron

41. GOODFELLAS Screenplay by Nicholas Pileggi & Martin Scorsese. Based on book "Wise Guy" by Nicholas Pileggi

42. RAIDERS OF THE LOST ARK Screenplay by Lawrence Kasdan. Story by George Lucas and Philip Kaufman

43. TAXI DRIVER Written by Paul Schrader

44. THE BEST YEARS OF OUR LIVES Screenplay by Robert E. Sherwood. Based on novel "Glory For Me" by MacKinley Kantor

45. ONE FLEW OVER THE CUCKOO'S NEST Screenplay by Lawrence Hauben and Bo Goldman. Based on the novel by Ken Kesey

46. THE TREASURE OF THE SIERRA MADRE Screenplay by John Huston. Based on the novel by B. Traven

47. THE MALTESE FALCON Screenplay by John Huston. Based on the novel by Dashiell Hammett

48. THE BRIDGE ON THE RIVER KWAI Screenplay by Carl Foreman and Michael Wilson. Based on the novel by Pierre Boulle

49. SCHINDLER'S LIST Screenplay by Steven Zaillian. Based on the novel by Thomas Keneally

50. THE SIXTH SENSE Written by M. Night Shyamalan

51. BROADCAST NEWS Written by James L. Brooks

52. THE LADY EVE Screenplay by Preston Sturges. Story by Monckton Hoffe

53. ALL THE PRESIDENT'S MEN Screenplay by William Goldman. Based on the book by Carl Bernstein & Bob Woodward

54. MANHATTAN Written by Woody Allen & Marshall Brickman

55. APOCALYPSE NOW Written by John Milius and Francis Coppola. Narration by Michael Herr

56. BACK TO THE FUTURE Written by Robert Zemeckis & Bob Gale

57. CRIMES AND MISDEMEANORS Written by Woody Allen

58. ORDINARY PEOPLE Screenplay by Alvin Sargent. Based on the novel by Judith Guest

59. IT HAPPENED ONE NIGHT Screenplay by Robert Riskin. Based on the story "Night Bus" by Samuel Hopkins Adams

60. L.A. CONFIDENTIAL Screenplay by Brian Helgeland & Curtis Hanson. Based on the novel by James Ellroy

61. THE SILENCE OF THE LAMBS Screenplay by Ted Tally. Based on the novel by Thomas Harris

62. MOONSTRUCK Written by John Patrick Shanley

63. JAWS Screenplay by Peter Benchley and Carl Gottlieb. Based on the novel by Peter Benchley

64. TERMS OF ENDEARMENT Screenplay by James L. Brooks. Based on the novel by Larry McMurtry

65. SINGIN' IN THE RAIN Screen Story and Screenplay by Betty Comden & Adolph Green. Based on the song by Arthur Freed and Nacio Herb Brown

66. JERRY MAGUIRE Written by Cameron Crowe

67. E.T. THE EXTRA-TERRESTRIAL Written by Melissa Mathison

68. STAR WARS Written by George Lucas

69. DOG DAY AFTERNOON Screenplay by Frank Pierson. Based on a magazine article by P.F. Kluge and Thomas Moore

70. THE AFRICAN QUEEN Screenplay by James Agee and John Huston. Based on the novel by C.S. Forester

71. THE LION IN WINTER Screenplay by James Goldman. Based on the play by James Goldman

72. THELMA & LOUISE Written by Callie Khouri

73. AMADEUS Screenplay by Peter Shaffer. Based on his play

74. BEING JOHN MALKOVICH Written by Charlie Kaufman

75. HIGH NOON Screenplay by Carl Foreman. Based on short story "The Tin Star" by John W. Cunningham

76. RAGING BULL Screenplay by Paul Schrader and Mardik Martin. Based on the book by Jake La Motta with Joseph Carter and Peter Savage

77. ADAPTATION Screenplay by Charlie Kaufman and Donald Kaufman. Based on the book "The Orchid Thief" by Susan Orlean

78. ROCKY Written by Sylvester Stallone

79. THE PRODUCERS Written by Mel Brooks

80. WITNESS Screenplay by Earl W. Wallace & William Kelley. Story by William Kelley and Pamela Wallace & Earl W. Wallace

81. BEING THERE Screenplay by Jerzy Kosinski. Inspired by the novel by Jerzy Kosinski

82. COOL HAND LUKE Screenplay by Donn Pearce and Frank Pierson. Based on the novel by Donn Pearce

83. REAR WINDOW Screenplay by John Michael Hayes. Based on the short story by Cornell Woolrich

84. THE PRINCESS BRIDE Screenplay by William Goldman. Based on his novel

85. LA GRANDE ILLUSION Written by Jean Renoir and Charles Spaak

86. HAROLD & MAUDE Written by Colin Higgins

87. 8 1/2 Screenplay by Federico Fellini, Tullio Pinelli, Ennio Flaiano, Brunello Rond. Story by Fellini, Flaiano

88. FIELD OF DREAMS Screenplay by Phil Alden Robinson. Based on the book by W.P. Kinsella

89. FORREST GUMP Screenplay by Eric Roth. Based on the novel by Winston Groom

90. SIDEWAYS Screenplay by Alexander Payne & Jim Taylor. Based on the novel by Rex Pickett

91. THE VERDICT Screenplay by David Mamet. Based on the novel by Barry Reed

92. PSYCHO Screenplay by Joseph Stefano. Based on the novel by Robert Bloch

93. DO THE RIGHT THING Written by Spike Lee

94. PATTON Screen Story and Screenplay by Francis Ford Coppola and Edmund H. North. Based on "A Soldier's Story" by Omar H. Bradley and "Patton: Ordeal and Triumph" by Ladislas Farago

95. HANNAH AND HER SISTERS Written by Woody Allen

96. THE HUSTLER Screenplay by Sidney Carroll & Robert Rossen. Based on the novel by Walter Tevis

97. THE SEARCHERS Screenplay by Frank S. Nugent. Based on the novel by Alan Le May

98. THE GRAPES OF WRATH Screenplay by Nunnally Johnson. Based on the novel by John Steinbeck

99. THE WILD BUNCH Screenplay by Walon Green and Sam Peckinpah. Story by Walon Green and Roy Sickner

100. MEMENTO Screenplay by Christopher Nolan. Based on the short story "Memento Mori" by Jonathan Nolan

101. NOTORIOUS Written by Ben Hecht

LINDA BERGMAN
FILM CREDITS

(Status)

WRITER – *THE GRAND BABY*, feature film (in development)

PRODUCER/WRITER – *NOT DEAD YET!*, feature film (in development)

PRODUCER/WRITER – *TOOT, TOOT, TOOTSIE, GOODBYE*, feature film, co-written with Martin Tahse (in development)

PRODUCER/WRITER – *FORSYTHE*, Series Pilot, Peak Entertainment

WRITER – *ANATOMY OF A SHOPLIFTER*, 2hr ABC, Lifetime, Frank and Bob Films

PRODUCER/WRITER – *CHINA'S PEARL*, 3hr ABC, Valerie Harper/Tony Cacciotti, Exec. Producers

WRITER – *THE LIFE*, 2hr CBS Kathryn Petri, Michael Wright, Execs.

WRITER – *A WOMAN'S PLACE*, 2hr Lifetime TV, Hearst Entertainment, starring Lorraine Bracco

WRITER – *FAMILY AFFAIR*, 2hr Lifetime TV, Hearst Entertainment

PRODUCER/WRITER – *A FATHER'S SON – THE MICHAEL LANDON STORY*, 2hr Green/Epstein Productions for CBS, starring John Schneider

WRITER – *THE PRINCESS CLUB*, 2hr Robert Greenwald Productions/ CBS

PRODUCER/WRITER – *GET TO THE HEART: THE BARBARA MANDRELL STORY*, 2hr Mandalay Films/CBS

WRITER – *THE GLASS COCKPIT*, 2hr Mandalay Films/CBS

WRITER – *HIGHJACK*, 1hr episode, "ORLEANS" John Sacret Young, Executive Producer, starring Larry Hagman

WRITER – *DARK VISIONS*, 2hr Republic Films/ABC

WRITER – *ALMOST GOLDEN: THE JESSICA SAVITCH STORY*, 2hr Lifetime starring Sela Ward, Ron Silver

WRITER – *THE JANET HOLLEY STORY*, 2hr CBS, Jaffe-Braunstein Productions, starring Janine Turner

WRITER – *ON THEIR OWN:WOMEN IN PRISON*, 2hr ABC starring Judith Light, Stacy Keach

PRODUCER/WRITER – *KISS MY LILIES*, 1hr pilot NBC, Brian Pike Productions

PRODUCER/WRITER – *RIO SHANNON,* 2hr pilot ABC starring Blair Brown, Michael DeLuise and Penny Fuller; John Sacret Young, Exec. Prod., Mimi Leder, director

CO-PRODUCER/ WRITER – *MATTERS OF THE HEART,* 2hr USA Network, Jane Seymour, Christopher Gartin, (**Writer's Guild Award Nominee**) (**Media Access Award**)

CO-WRITER – *THE LOOKALIKE,* 2hr USA starring Melissa Gilbert, Diane Ladd, Lillian Gallo Productions

CO-WRITER – *JUST TIPSY, HONEY*, 1hr ABC After School Special

WRITER – *WANNA PLAY?* – 1hr musical special, PBS, **Alpha Award winner** for excellence in children's programming

For more information about
Linda Bergman and how
to contact her, visit her website at:
www.soyouthinkyourlifesamovie.com